DAVID PETRAEUS

DAVID PETRAEUS

A Biography

Bradley T. Gericke

GREENWOOD BIOGRAPHIES

 GREENWOOD

AN IMPRINT OF ABC-CLIO, LLC
Santa Barbara, California • Denver, Colorado • Oxford, England

Library of Congress Cataloging-in-Publication Data

Gericke, Bradley T.

   David Petraeus : a biography / Bradley T. Gericke.
      p. cm. — (Greenwood biographies)
   Includes bibliographical references and index.
   ISBN 978-0-313-38377-9 (hard copy : alk. paper) — ISBN 978-0-313-38378-6
(ebook) 1. Petraeus, David Howell. 2. Generals—United States—
Biography. 3. United States. Army—Biography. 4. Iraq War, 2003—
Biography. I. Title.
   E897.4.P48G47 2011
   355.0092—dc22   2010032467
   [B]

ISBN: 978-0-313-38377-9
EISBN: 978-0-313-38378-6

15   14   13   12   2   3   4   5

This book is also available on the World Wide Web as an eBook.
Visit www.abc-clio.com for details.

Greenwood
An Imprint of ABC-CLIO, LLC

ABC-CLIO, LLC
130 Cremona Drive, P.O. Box 1911
Santa Barbara, California 93116-1911

This book is printed on acid-free paper ∞

Manufactured in the United States of America

To the soldiers of the U.S. Army,
who have been defending America and the cause
of freedom since 1775.

CONTENTS

SERIES FOREWORD

In response to high school and public library needs, Greenwood developed this distinguished series of full-length biographies specifically for student use. Prepared by field experts and professionals, these engaging biographies are tailored for high school students who need challenging yet accessible biographies. Ideal for secondary school assignments, the length, format and subject areas are designed to meet educators' requirements and students' interests.

Greenwood offers an extensive selection of biographies spanning all curriculum related subject areas including social studies, the sciences, literature and the arts, history and politics, as well as popular culture, covering public figures and famous personalities from all time periods and backgrounds, both historic and contemporary, who have made an impact on American and/or world culture. Greenwood biographies were chosen based on comprehensive feedback from librarians and educators. Consideration was given to both curriculum relevance and inherent interest. The result is an intriguing mix of the well known and the unexpected, the saints and sinners from long-ago history and contemporary pop culture. Readers will find a wide array of subject choices from fascinating crime figures like Al Capone to inspiring pioneers like Margaret Mead, from the greatest minds of our time like Stephen Hawking to the most amazing success stories of our day like J. K. Rowling.

While the emphasis is on fact, not glorification, the books are meant to be fun to read. Each volume provides in-depth information about the subject's life from birth through childhood, the teen years, and adulthood. A thorough account relates family background and education, traces personal and professional influences, and explores struggles, accomplishments, and contributions. A timeline highlights the most significant life events against a historical perspective. Bibliographies supplement the reference value of each volume.

PREFACE

When General David Howell Petraeus tells the story, he leans forward just a bit, tensing his shoulders, his lean frame as unyielding as the sharp tone of his voice. He believes in the importance of this moment: Late on a rain-soaked night in April 1862, the fate of the American republic, that great gift bestowed by the generation that fought and won the Revolutionary War, hung in the balance. General Ulysses S. Grant, commander of the Union forces in south central Tennessee, couldn't—or wouldn't—sleep. His troops had been bloodied all day in the fields and woods surrounding Shiloh church. A Confederate attack at sunrise had surprised him and nearly pushed his men into the river that ran only yards behind where he now leaned against a bullet-scarred tree. The fight had been that close. He had nearly lost his entire army, and, while reinforcements were arriving, the outcome of the battle was unsure. Even now, in the darkness, his weary soldiers were struggling to reform their lines, the wounded stumbling and crying, the dead silent but irreplaceable. Most leaders would have shrunk from the prospect of more fighting in these conditions. Most would reason that pulling back, regrouping, doing anything but holding that tenuous position was the thing to do. Fortunately for the Union, Grant was not like most officers. When Grant's chief lieutenant, William T. Sherman, found his boss late in the night, Grant was peering into the gloom of a terrific rainstorm, his teeth clenched on a soggy cigar. "Well, Grant, we've had the devil's own day, haven't we?" he said. Without hesitation came Grant's reply: "Yep. Lick 'em tomorrow, though."

When Petraeus repeats Grant's determined response, he pauses for just a second, taking in the quiet audacity of Grant's figure in that rain swept moment of 150 years ago. Petraeus wants and expects his listener to understand, to really know, how decisive steady commanders in moments of crisis can be. Leaders are game changers. Leaders make history. Petraeus knows it, and he draws inspiration from Grant's example, because he is constantly mining the past for lessons to be learned. It is this intellectual curiosity, coupled with his extraordinary determination and a clear-eyed sense for the nature of warfare, that makes him a unique general. Petraeus, like Grant, came to his knowledge through dedicated study for sure, but also through the grinding trial of experience, which taught him both the limitations and the possibilities that one can create in war. Petraeus wouldn't say it out loud, but all these things make him, in fact, much like Grant, a man seeking victory on the battlefield even as he is propelled forward to bigger and broader roles, all the way to the highest military and national stages. The two leaders come from different times of American history, and reflect different backgrounds, but Grant and Petraeus share a relentless intensity to prevail in war, a trait that sets the two men apart.

Historians often debate the causes and catalysts that propel the course of human events, especially questions surrounding how and why wars are won and lost. Do wars begin and end due to grand reasons? Or can individual leaders shape history? Can any single person really change the direction of his time? The record of General David Petraeus will no doubt be examined in light of these questions.

When the cold war ended with the dissolution of the Soviet Union in the early 1990s, America's armed forces, especially the U.S. Army, were somewhat adrift. Since World War II, some 50 years earlier, the U.S. Army had trained and organized itself to fight a large war against Soviet and Warsaw Pact armies in central Europe. Its most important and expensive weapons were M1 Abrams battle tanks, mechanized 155 mm artillery howitzers, Apache attack helicopters, and infantry who rode into battle on high-speed Bradley fighting vehicles. But suddenly, this kind of war appeared less likely. Except for the Gulf War in 1991, the army, and its sister services, found itself deploying to conduct more localized contingencies, such as those in Somalia and the Balkans. Deciding which equipment to purchase, how to train soldiers, and just how to think about war posed a real problem for army leaders.

Then the terrorist attacks of September 11, 2001, changed everything again. Now the army knew that it would have to fight a new kind of enemy, and likely for many years to come. Petraeus, by being ahead of his peers in the way he had prepared himself professionally, was suited to adapt to the new environment. There is no doubt that he has benefited from the fortuitous coincidence of rising to high rank at just the moment when his many years of study of the nature of irregular, or small wars, and his distinct grasp of how to navigate America's mainstream media and national political environments were most in demand. Yet Petraeus must be given credit for being prepared for just such an opportunity. Both through the assignments with officers senior to himself, the civilian graduate education he sought for himself, and his persistent belief that the United States must be prepared to wage war that was something short of the massive conventional fight that seemed likely during the cold war decades, Petraeus was ready to seize his moment when it arrived.

Petraeus combines tactical and technical excellence with the keen ability, sometimes directly, sometimes through a cadre of staff members and loyal advisors, to cultivate the policy and media establishment of Washington, D.C. Petraeus is irrepressibly candid, but he is far from open. He is always on message. Within the Department of Defense, and especially the army where he was more familiar, Petraeus is still the tough and striving competitor progressing through the officer ranks, of which he has long been a member. He is also the face of a call for the American military establishment to transform the way its forces are trained and organized. Today, military staffs across the Pentagon have taken note of his successes and are working to understand the emerging trends of the international security environment so that U.S. forces can fight and win in this complex security environment.

On the international stage, he is the preeminent uniformed figure of the United States. As commander of coalition forces in Iraq and later as the commanding general of U.S. Central Command, and subsequently

General David Petraeus is the most momentous military leader of his generation. While his leadership in Iraq would prove decisive, his impact on American military doctrine and culture may be his most important legacy. AP Photo/Khalid Mohammed

leader of the U.S. war in Afghanistan, responsible for American forces throughout the Middle East, his public star burns brighter than that of his peers. He fought alongside other U.S. commanders, of course, but it is he who is first credited with restoring confidence in America after the dismay prompted by the difficulties of the early years of the war in Iraq. His renown comes most assuredly because of his accomplishments related to Iraq, whether turning the tide on the ground or decisively engaging Congress in testimony at home, but also because more broadly he suits the role that popular opinion demands of successful military leaders.

The core attribute that the public wants from its generals is success on the battlefield. They expect that the treasure of their sons and daughters will be safely guarded, and that senior commanders will lead with dignity and determination. Petraeus does this in spades—his style is perseverance writ large. And by managing his public persona as skillfully as he manages his professional affairs, Petraeus has become an icon of popular culture and a household name. By doing so, he has joined the ranks of the military greats of American history. Where he will ultimately rank remains an unanswered question. History will tell.

Petraeus has his own gesture to communicate his respect for the vagaries of circumstance—he often concludes his responses to queries with a sharp rap on the table, and the words *touch wood*. So when testifying to the Senate, Petraeus responds, "Touch wood, that's on track." To an interviewer, he instructs, "Touch wood on that, if you please." It's a habit he repeats publicly probably a hundred times a year and even more frequently when guiding his staff. It reminds both him and his listener that nobody is master of the future. History must be given its due. The complexity that characterizes human behavior must be respected. Petraeus knows that when he cannot control an event, he must observe it and interrogate it, and only then respond aggressively once again.

As General Petraeus is still an actively serving military officer, there is neither memoir nor archive of his papers, and in fact, many of the details about his actions and decisions remain classified. However, public sources, especially interviews by journalists, are plentiful. I have thus researched only publicly available, unclassified secondary sources. All citations appear from such works. Chief among my full-length sources have been Thomas Ricks's often-critical books, *The Fiasco* (Penguin Press, 2006) and *The Gamble* (Penguin Press, 2009); the much more conciliatory *Tell Me How This Ends*, by Linda Robinson (PublicAffairs, 2008); and the book that more closely captures Petraeus's persona, *The Fourth Star*, by Greg Jaffe and David Cloud (Crown, 2009). Finally, the recent articles by Mark Bowden in *Vanity Fair*, "David Petraeus's Winning Streak" and "The Professor of War" (2010), contain insights not found in any of the longer works.

I must note that while I have had the privilege to serve for a short while in General Petraeus's command, I have avoided inclusion of any fact in this biography that derives from my personal experiences. Instead, I have overwhelmingly relied upon published sources, and, in a few cases, the observations of participants in the events discussed. All interpretations are solely my own and do not reflect the positions of the U.S. Army nor the Department of Defense.

I would foremost like to thank my wife, Tonya, an extraordinary woman of intrepid character who is a constant pillar of resolve in all things, personal and professional. Through the years, she has selflessly dedicated herself time and again in support of my military and academic pursuits. I wish to acknowledge my parents as well, who instilled in me a passion for history, and supported my decision to pursue an army career.

I also owe a hearty thank you to my colleagues and fellow officers who read drafts of this work and shared their valuable insights. And, of course, I extend my gratitude to Padraic (Pat) Carlin and the staff at Greenwood, who aided me with great professional poise at every step of the process of completing this book. Any errors remaining in the text are strictly my own.

TIMELINE: EVENTS IN THE LIFE OF DAVID PETRAEUS

Youth

7 Nov 1952   Born in Cornwall, New York

May 1974   Graduation from West Point, Commissioned Infantry branch

Professional Assignments

May 75–Jan 79   Platoon leader, C Company, later logistics officer (S4), later personnel officer (S1), 509th Airborne Battalion Combat Team, Vicenza, Italy

Jan 79–Jul 79   Assistant S3 (operations), 2d Brigade, 24th Infantry Division (Mechanized), Fort Stewart, Georgia

Jul 79–May 81   Commander, A Company, later S3 (operations), 2d Battalion, 19th Infantry, 24th Infantry Division (Mechanized), Fort Stewart, Georgia

May 81–May 82   Aide-de-camp to the division commander, 24th Infantry Division (Mechanized), Fort Stewart, Georgia

May 82–Jun 83	Student, Command and General Staff Officer Course, Fort Leavenworth, Kansas
Jun 83–Jun 85	Student, Princeton University, Princeton, New Jersey
Jul 85–Jun 87	Instructor, later assistant professor, Department of Social Sciences, United States Military Academy (USMA), West Point, New York
Jun 87–Jun 88	Military assistant to the supreme Allied commander Europe, Supreme Headquarters, Allied Powers Europe, Belgium
Jun 88–Aug 89	Operations officer (S3), 2d Battalion, 30th Infantry Regiment, later 1st Brigade, 3d Infantry Division (Mechanized), U.S. Army Europe, Germany
Aug 89–Aug 91	Aide/assistant executive officer to the chief of staff, U.S. Army, Washington, D.C.
Aug 91–Jul 93	Commander, 3d Battalion, 187th Infantry, 101st Airborne Division (Air Assault), Fort Campbell, Kentucky
Jul 93–Jul 94	G3 (operations)/director of Plans, Training and Mobilization, 101st Airborne Division (Air Assault), Fort Campbell, Kentucky
Aug 94–Jan 95	Senior service college fellow, Georgetown University, Washington, D.C.
Jan 95–Jun 95	Chief operations officer, UN Mission in Haiti, Operation Uphold Democracy, Haiti
Jun 95–Jun 97	Commander, 1st Brigade, 82d Airborne Division, Fort Bragg, North Carolina
Jun 97–Sep 97	Executive assistant to the director of the Joint Staff, the Joint Staff, Washington, D.C.
Oct 97–Aug 99	Executive assistant to the chairman, Joint Chiefs of Staff, Office of the Joint Chiefs of Staff, Washington, D.C.
Aug 99–Jul 00	Assistant division commander (operations), 82d Airborne Division, Fort Bragg, North Carolina; and commanding general, Combined Joint Task Force Kuwait, Operation Desert Spring, Kuwait

Jul 00–Aug 00	Acting commanding general, 82d Airborne Division, Fort Bragg, North Carolina
Aug 00–Jun 01	Chief of staff, XVIII Airborne Corps, Fort Bragg, North Carolina
Jun 01–Jun 02	Assistant chief of staff for operations, SFOR and deputy commander, U.S. Joint Interagency Counter Terrorism Task Force, Operation Joint Forge, Sarajevo, Bosnia Herzegovina
Jul 02–May 04	Commanding general, 101st Airborne Division (Air Assault) and Fort Campbell, Fort Campbell, Kentucky; and Operation Iraqi Freedom, Iraq
May 04–Sep 05	Commander, Multi-National Security Transition Command Iraq, NATO Training Mission Iraq, Operation Iraqi Freedom, Iraq
Oct 05–Feb 07	Commanding general, U.S. Army Combined Arms Center and Fort Leavenworth, Fort Leavenworth, Kansas
Feb 07–Sep 08	Commander, Multi-National Force Iraq, Operation Iraqi Freedom, Iraq
Oct 08–Present	Commander, U.S. Central Command, MacDill Air Force Base, Florida

Educational Degrees

USMA—BS—No Major
Princeton University—MPA—Public and International Affairs
Princeton University—PhD—International Relations

Military Schools Attended

Infantry Officer Basic and Advanced Courses
Armor Officer Advanced Course
U.S. Army Command and General Staff College
Senior Service College Fellowship Georgetown University

Promotions, Date of Appointment

2d Lieutenant	5 Jun 1974
1st Lieutenant	5 Jun 1976
Captain	8 Aug 1978
Major	1 Aug 1985
Lieutenant colonel	1 Apr 1991
Colonel	1 Sep 1995
Brigadier general	1 Jan 2000
Major general	1 Jan 2003
Lieutenant general	18 May 2004
General	10 Feb 2007

U.S. Decorations and Badges

Defense Distinguished Service Medal (with Oak Leaf Cluster)
Distinguished Service Medal (with Oak Leaf Cluster)
Defense Superior Service Medal (with Oak Leaf Cluster)
Legion of Merit (with three Oak Leaf Clusters)
Bronze Star Medal with V Device
Defense Meritorious Service Medal
Meritorious Service Medal (with two Oak Leaf Clusters)
Joint Service Commendation Medal
Army Commendation Medal (with two Oak Leaf Clusters)
Joint Service Achievement Medal
Army Achievement Medal
Combat Action Badge
Expert Infantryman Badge
Master Parachutist Badge
Air Assault Badge
Ranger Tab
Joint Chiefs of Staff Identification Badge
Army Staff Identification Badge

Key Dates of the Iraq War

October 2002 U.S. Congress authorizes President Bush to use military force against Iraq.

March 2003	UN weapons inspectors evacuate Iraq; U.S.-led Coalition invades Iraq.
April 2003	Iraqi regime of Saddam Hussein collapses.
May 2003	Coalition Provisional Authority is established.
December 2003	Saddam Hussein is captured.
April 2004	Uprising by Shiite cleric Moqtada al-Sadr begins in Baghdad and southern Iraq.
June 2004	An interim Iraqi government assumes control, and elections are planned.
January 2005	Iraqis elect a National Assembly; Shiites win a majority; Sunnis largely boycott.
April 2005	The National Assembly selects a president and prime minister.
October 2005	Saddam Hussein's trial begins.
December 2005	Iraq holds parliamentary elections.
February 2006	The Shiite Golden Mosque in Samarra is bombed; widespread violence ensues.
May 2006	Nouri al-Maliki becomes prime minister.
December 2006	Saddam Hussein is executed.
January 2007	President Bush announces a surge of more than 20,000 troops to be sent to Iraq.
September 2007	General Petraeus reports to Congress on the state of the war.
April 2008	General Petraeus again briefs Congress, and General Raymond Odierno is selected to succeed Petraeus as commander of forces in Iraq.
November 2008	Iraq's government calls for U.S. forces to withdraw by 2011.
January 2009	Iraqis assume control of portions of the Green Zone in Baghdad; the massive new U.S. embassy opens; Iraq holds nationwide elections.
March 2009	President Obama announces that U.S. forces will be reduced to 50,000 and the end of combat mission by August 31, 2010.
May 2009	The United Kingdom ends its operations in Iraq; the few remaining forces from other Coalition states soon depart as well.

June 2009	U.S. forces withdraw from Iraq's cities.
March 2010	Iraq holds parliamentary elections.

Key Dates of the Afghanistan War

1996	Taliban seizes control of Afghanistan's national government and introduces hard-line version of Islam.
August 1998	U.S. launches cruise missiles at suspected bases of militant Osama bin Laden.
October 2001	United States, United Kingdom launch strikes against Taliban targets.
November 2001	Taliban forces retreat after attacks by Northern Alliance and U.S. special operations troops
March 2002	Operation Anaconda begins.
June 2002	Loya Jirga, or Grand Council, elects Hamid Karzai as interim head of state.
August 2003	NATO assumes control of security in Kabul.
January 2004	Loya Jirga adopts new constitution.
October–November 2004	Hamid Karzai wins presidential elections.
September 2005	First parliamentary and provincial elections in more than three decades are held.
October 2006	NATO assumes responsibility for security across the whole of Afghanistan.
September 2008	President Bush sends an additional 4,500 U.S. troops.
February–March 2009	United States announces additional forces totaling more than 20,000 troops and a new strategy for Afghanistan.
May 2009	Stanley McChrystal is appointed new U.S. commander.
August 2009	Presidential and provincial elections are held but are marred by fraud.
September 2009	General McChrystal's report calling for more forces is leaked publicly.

October 2009	Hamid Karzai is declared winner of the election.
December 2009	President Obama orders 30,000 more troops to Afghanistan.
July, 2010	General Petraeus assumes command in Afghanistan.

Chapter 1

BOYHOOD IN NEW YORK

The life of David Howell Petraeus began in the way that so many American lives of consequence do, that is, in relative obscurity. Petraeus was born November 7, 1952, in the quiet town of Cornwall, New York, and would spend his youth in the adjacent historic community of Cornwall-on-Hudson, a village of several thousand souls nestled amid the historic peaks of the Hudson Highlands, an hour's drive north of New York City and only several miles from the United States Military Academy (USMA) at West Point. Although distant from the academy only by the looming presence of Storm King Mountain, the daily rhythms of the sleepy riverfront community were a world apart from the far-ranging interests of the eager cadets and faculty who hailed from across the United States and whose ranks Petraeus would eventually join and stand out among.

Petraeus's father, Sixtus, had been a Dutch merchant marine captain who immigrated to the United States when the Nazis overran Holland in 1940. He sailed with the U.S. Merchant Marine during the war and then, upon the return of peace, worked for a local power utility. Sixtus, who was a colorful, brave, and worldly character in contrast to many of the other fathers in town, took an active role in the young Petraeus's life, coaching several sports teams. From his earliest years, Petraeus, although lean and wiry, demonstrated a keen competitive streak that would inform his behavior as an adult. He coupled his natural athletic ability as a terrific endurance runner with an unrelenting drive to win and to become a star athlete on local teams. The local kids gave Petraeus the nickname "Peaches," an affectionate label that was easier for young tongues than his real last name. While it was a name that would stick with him as an adult, of course, not many would be brave enough to utter it later in the presence of the general.

His mother, Miriam Howell Petraeus, a graduate from Oberlin college at a time when it was still unique for a woman in middle America to possess formal education beyond secondary schooling, looked upon learning fondly and impressed in her son a lifetime affection for knowledge. Their home contained hundreds of books, which Petraeus avidly read when not leading the neighborhood group of boys in youthful mischief. Although his family had no particular military ties, like all of the kids in town, Petraeus knew much about the military academy on the other side of the mountain. More than once, he and his friends had to be ordered away from the academy's athletic fields where Petraeus was leading pickup games. Whether it was running or hiking or skiing in the winter, Petraeus viewed West Point and the always-hurrying cadets he frequently encountered with a fair degree of wide-eyed wonderment.

The people of Cornwall-on-Hudson experienced their share of the tremors of the social and political revolutions that swept the country in the 1950s and 1960s, but they were relatively isolated from, and no doubt unsympathetic to, much of the protest that riled larger towns and cities across the country during the Vietnam War. Petraeus's boyhood was thus filled with the echoes of Vietnam. However, it was the retired officers and military veterans who lived in the area who were the visible and inspiring reminders of a much wider world whose influence reached very nearby and could ultimately be the avenue for an enterprising young man in search of bigger challenges.

In high school, Petraeus began thinking about where he would go after graduation. College was definitely on the horizon, and as a star soccer player and excellent student, the army officers who lived in town sought to recruit him. Later, Petraeus would say, "A lot of life, I think, is about trying to be like people you think highly of." Seeing and talking to veterans who were among his coaches and teachers worked on Petraeus's imagination. As he noted, he was also drawn to the "idea of service to something larger than oneself," a sentiment that has unified generations of young Americans from all walks of life who attend West Point.[1]

His mother wasn't so sure the academy was the best place for her son. She preferred Colgate University, a place more like her Oberlin and for which Petraeus had been recruited for his academic and soccer achievements. Besides, Vietnam was still raging, and it seemed likely that her boy would be sent there when he graduated in four years. But the family's income was modest, and when USMA offered Petraeus the opportunity to join the soccer team, the lure of a tuition-free education and the knowledge that as a cadet, Petraeus could still drop out anytime during his first two years, proved tempting. There was no doubt, however, that the chief lure was the opportunity to serve and be part of something much larger than himself; that was the deciding factor in Petraeus's decision. He had the talent and drive to succeed in any number of endeavors, but Petraeus chose West Point.

NOTE

1. Linda Robinson, *Tell Me How This Ends* (New York: Public Affairs, 2008), 51.

Chapter 2

THE FIRST CRUCIBLE: WEST POINT

In early July of 1970, Petraeus bid farewell to his parents and was immediately consumed in the summer-long training regime for new cadets, affectionately known by the upperclassmen as Beast Barracks. This first summer at the academy was the army's version of the timeless ritual that turned young men, most unfamiliar with military culture and hailing from thoroughly civilian backgrounds, into cadets who would eventually become officers—not just soldiers, but leaders of soldiers. In the course of six demanding weeks, the new cadets (they were not full-fledged cadets until they graduated from Beast in August) were taught to forget nearly everything about their former lives as high school all-stars, class presidents, and church leaders. Now strident upperclassman hectored Petraeus and his peers to learn West Point's way of performing even the most mundane tasks. New cadets were told how to march (eyes ahead, 30-inch steps), how to eat (silently, small bites and utensils resting on the plate's edge), how to keep their rooms and make their beds (everything perfectly aligned, and the bed sheets drawn tight), and how to walk to class (in a rapid walk, or pinging step). New cadets were even told how to speak: They were permitted only four authorized answers to any question, "Yes sir: no sir: no excuse sir: and sir, I do not understand." A new cadet who replied differently could be expected to incur the wrath of an upper-classman.

Many of the rules and regulations endured by new cadets were silliness and included a degree of hazing, but there were important purposes behind the indoctrination. The culture of the academy was designed to build teamwork and cohesion among the cadets by teaching them that their individual wants and needs were subordinate to the higher purposes of the army. As their individual identities were diminished in a sea of conformity and cadet gray, they were learning how to follow, a fundamental experience they had to thoroughly understand before they could try their hands at greater responsibilities. In war, they would be responsible for the lives of their soldiers and so now they learned that there could be no excuse for failure, even of the most minor detail. Drilled into them was the fact that in combat, success means not only accomplishing the mission but is also a matter of life and death. Alertness, determination, and loyalty would lead to success while at the academy and during a career in the army. Petraeus passed every one of these initial tests, quickly adapting to the rigors of cadet life.

The changes that would end the draft in America were still several years away, and the army was rocked by the turmoil surrounding the drawdown from Vietnam, which riled the force, including its training establishment and West Point. The upper-class cadets sometimes reflected the force's anxieties through acts of petty tyranny. While it was a stressful experience, as a plebe, or freshman, Petraeus paid close attention to the details of every task at hand and led his peers in finding ways to bond together to succeed. He finished the plebe year with a high standing in his class, earning mostly a mix of As and Bs. His class rank, which included evaluation of his military and physical training performance, was 161st out of more than 800 classmates, an excellent performance, but one that Petraeus was determined to improve upon.

Emerging from the trials and tribulations of life as a plebe, Petraeus hit his stride as a sophomore, or yearling, as second-year cadets are described in the language cadets use with one another. West Point is an ascetic place, an atmosphere that rewards a monkish lifestyle, hard work, and relentless striving for success. A powerful sense of purpose infuses West Point. Founded in 1802, the academy is the nation's oldest, and its graduates take its role as defender of the nation in every conflict since very seriously. Even in times of peace, West Point graduates have done their part to shape the country as engineers, explorers, and business leaders. Even its color bespeaks gravity: the uniforms are gray, the buildings are gray, and for months in winter, known by cadets as the gloom period, even the skies are sullenly gray. It was a place and a way of viewing life as an important and profound journey to be studied and ultimately mastered that suited cadet Petraeus. And he enjoyed being surrounded by others like him with whom he could compete—bright, energetic, and top-notch performers. Petraeus even turned his habit of long-distance running into a personal means of demonstrating his superiority over his peers. Running with friends became a way to show others that he would not allow himself to be the one who fell behind or to show any sign of weakness.

Petraeus thrived in a system of incessant grading and detailed regulation that the staff and faculty imposed upon the cadets. They were—and still are—scored for their conduct in ways that civilians would consider remarkably intrusive but that Petraeus and his peers learned to expect. Every day, the army officers of the Brigade Tactical Department scored the cadets in dozens of ways. They inspected cadets' rooms; assessed how the cadets performed duties around the barracks, how they marched during hours of drill and ceremony, and how well they could shoot their rifles; and several times a year, put the cadets through physical-training exams, including the famously difficult indoor obstacle course. Some cadets sought ways to game the system, and Petraeus did his share to maximize his efficiency. He knew all manner of tricks to keep his shoes to a gleaming shine and his uniform looking sharp. But for Petraeus, the marks awarded for every aspect of cadet life were indicators of his performance and provided opportunities to compete. There were rarely enough hours in the day for him—he played varsity sports three seasons a year and studied hard. Petraeus was a serious cadet. He didn't much fool around, didn't go to many movies, and didn't hang out with other cadets who often could be found lounging at the social center in Grant Hall. Petraeus was rewarded for his exertions by being awarded a gold star on his collar, marking him as a star man—a privilege reserved for the top 5 percent of each class.

As an upperclassman, Petraeus shined. Until midway through his senior year, he sought admission to medical school, an opportunity the academy was offering for a very select few cadets with superb grades who could be expected to reflect well upon the academy. But after earning a slot in the program, he realized that medical school was not for him and reset his focus on the opportunities to be found as a regular officer in the army. His performance was noted by his tactical officers who supervised cadets in their barracks, resulting in Petraeus earning a position as a cadet captain on the brigade staff. His promotion to relatively high cadet rank entailed significant leadership responsibility and was a duty given only to the top echelon of upper-class cadets.

Petraeus got along well with his classmates even if he wasn't particularly warm to many. His peers respected him and couldn't help but notice his proficiency to accomplish whatever he set out to do. Petraeus befriended his mates widely, although he was too reserved to be wildly popular. Next to his senior photo in the *Howitzer,* the annual cadet yearbook, a fellow cadet who had been his roommate portrayed Petraeus's single-mindedness: "Peaches came to the Mil Acad with high ambitions, but unlike most, he accomplished his goals. A striver to the Max, Dave was always 'going for it' in sport, academics, leadership, and even his social life. This attitude will surely lead to success in the future, Army or otherwise."[1]

Like most cadets, Petraeus underwent innumerable daily challenges and aggravations associated with the Spartan life of a cadet. And like cadets before and since, he drew daily inspiration from his surroundings to ease the daily frustrations and sense of purposelessness that many cadet tasks seemed to entail. Located amid soaring, wooded mountainsides, West Point looked and felt like the military fortress it was when first laid out as defensive works to protect George Washington's Continental army during the American Revolution. Although thoroughly modernized within, the majestic gray stone buildings couldn't help but instill a sense of fortitude and timeliness to the place. Martial statuary extolling the academy's greatest graduates who went on to lead American armies in war dotted the open spaces between barracks and classrooms, providing inescapable reminders of West Point's motto—Duty, Honor, Country—to cadets who walked by. But cadets had more than granite and marble visages to remind them of the responsibility they would assume as officers after graduation. Living heroes were present too. Veterans from Vietnam, and even men who served in the Korean War and during World

War II, frequently appeared at the academy. Some provided guest lectures, others mingled with cadets at football tailgates, and a number were on the faculty. One such person was Bill Carpenter, West Point's "Lonely End" football great who earned all-American honors and then served in Vietnam, earning a Distinguished Service Cross for bravery under fire.

In the spring of 1974, Petraeus, who graduated 43d in his class, adopted the slogan, "Pride of the Corps, 74." This meant he would have the 43d choice for selecting the branch of the army in which he wanted to serve as a lieutenant. Petraeus had made up his mind and wanted to be an infantryman, the branch along with armor charged with meeting any enemy face-to-face on the battlefield. As a consequence, infantry, especially in the wake of the grueling combat in the jungles of Vietnam, was not a popular choice. Hence most of the cadets ahead of him picked branches with a more glamorous or comfortable career path, such as aviation or

The United States Military Academy at West Point, founded in 1802, continues to inspire some of America's brightest young men and women to serve as commissioned army officers. When Petraeus attended in the 1970s, the academy was adjusting to the post-Vietnam era. AP Photo/Mike Groll.

military intelligence. When Petraeus's turn to select his branch came during a class formation, he stood to declare in a clear voice, "Infantry!" His choice elicited applause from his peers, as he was only the second to ask to be a *grunt*, as infantry troops are fondly known by soldiers in the army.

Several weeks after graduation, Petraeus married Holly Knowlton, the daughter of West Point's superintendent, Lieutenant General William Knowlton. His courtship of Holly made for a notable part of his West Point experience, and Petraeus's classmates ribbed him incessantly for dating her. The fact that the romance began as a blind date made it all the more remarkable. Those who knew him realized the genuine affection that he felt for Holly, a formidable character in her own right.

The previous autumn, Holly had come from Dickinson College in Carlisle, Pennsylvania, where she was a senior, to West Point to visit her parents during a football weekend, always a major social occasion. The Supe, as her father was known, lived in one of the most signature buildings on post, the famous Quarters 100, a prominent 19th-century home. It was built by West Point's first superintendent, Colonel Sylvanus Thayer, who is known as the "Father of the Military Academy" for the wide ranging reforms he instituted that still exist today. Built in 1820 and located adjacent to the academy's main parade ground, which is named the Plain, Petraeus couldn't escape attention when he knocked on the backdoor to visit Holly. Fortunately for Petraeus, the cadet that a friend of her mother had intended Holly to meet couldn't get free, so she asked Petraeus, without explaining who the date was. When he learned he was going to take the Supe's daughter to the game, he was taken aback. Arriving at the game several days later, he asked Holly for the tickets, which he had been told by the Supe's aide she had. Unfortunately, it quickly dawned on both of them that neither had the tickets. Showing the kind of quick-thinking Petraeus was known for, he kept his composure and bluffed his way past the gate officials and escorted Holly to the cadet section—where he tried to be low-key with his high-ranking date and where tickets weren't needed anyway, since the Corps of Cadets stood for the entire game.

Holly was a talented scholar in her own right, crafting her honors dissertation about French author and 1952 Nobel laureate François Mauriac. Fluent in French, she was attractive, smart, and ambitious and would graduate summa cum laude. When it came to dating Petraeus, she no doubt had the upper hand, but the two were quickly smitten. It became a frequent sight to see them together walking along the post's parklike setting or playing tennis. Importantly, Petraeus worked hard to stay on the good side of Holly's mother, Peggy, who soon considered him to be like another son in the family.

When Petraeus and Holly married on July 6, 1974, at West Point's magnificent Cadet Chapel, a gothic masterpiece located prominently on the hillside overlooking the Plain, he chose a bride who clearly understood the lifestyle of an army family. In fact, her military pedigree far exceeded his. Two of Holly's brothers were Vietnam War veterans. Her oldest brother had graduated from USMA just a few years before, also a star man. And her father, of course, was not only the superintendent but also a distinguished figure of the army. It was a time when most military families felt themselves isolated and at odds with much of the cultural turmoil going on beyond the gates of their installations. With the end of the draft and conversion to an all-volunteer armed services in 1973, the army had started on the course of becoming a professional force at every rank, but it would be a long transition before a new army that was respected by the public would emerge. For the moment, the disappointments and losses of the Vietnam War caused service members and their loved ones to feel isolated. General Knowlton, who saw it as his charge to uphold the academy during this tumultuous period, would exert a strong influence on Petraeus and serve as a role model of the kind of decisive, confident, and intellectually grounded leader the young officer aspired to be.

Knowlton, a West Point graduate, would ultimately retire in 1980 as a four-star general. His distinguished career began as a lieutenant in the armored cavalry during World War II. He earned a silver star for leading more than 60 of his troops through German lines to make contact with advancing Soviet elements. During the 1950s, he taught in the Social Science Department at West Point, and in 1957, he earned a master's degree in political science from Columbia University. In Vietnam, he advised General William Westmoreland about military-civil operations and was assistant division commander in the 9th Infantry Division. He also received two more Silver Stars. After four years as superintendent at

West Point, Knowlton returned to high-profile postings in Europe. He spent his final years on active duty as the U.S. representative to NATO's military committee in Brussels.

Petraeus studied Knowlton's career, noting the way his father-in-law exuded self-discipline and demonstrated an intelligent and cultivated combination of the attributes of both warrior and scholar. Over the years, the two would maintain a friendly repartee regarding their respective achievements as military leaders. Their relationship would be the first Petraeus would sustain with senior officers who shaped and molded his early years in the army.

NOTE

1. David Cloud and Greg Jaffe, *The Fourth Star* (New York: Crown Publishers), 17.

Chapter 3

JUNIOR OFFICER
YEARS IN THE ARMY

Fresh from West Point as a newly minted second lieutenant, Petraeus's first assignment was with the 509th Airborne Infantry battalion in Italy. But before he could assume his duties as a platoon leader, he first had to attend the Infantry Officer Basic Course (Petraeus was an honor graduate) and then, importantly, the Army Ranger course administered from Fort Benning, Georgia. The rangers are the army's elite light infantry force. They draw their heritage from the colonial militia unit organized by Major Thomas Rogers during the French and Indian War who undertook raids and performed reconnaissance and special missions in rugged and inhospitable terrain where regular troops could not operate effectively. In modern times, the rangers are known for their exploits under the most difficult circumstances, such as their assault up the cliffs of Point du Hoc during the Normandy invasion on June 6, 1944. Officers who want to advance in the infantry know that becoming a ranger is an important step.

The two-month course was grueling, but Petraeus stood out, winning all three top awards for the course: Distinguished Honor Graduate, reflecting the best overall performance in the course; the Darby Award, awarded for outstanding performance plus the highest peer ratings and not given in each course; and the Merrill's Marauder Award, for land navigation excellence. He could take satisfaction from his accomplishment because he had passed his first major test as an officer with flying colors. He felt especially gratified to win the last two awards because these reflected that he had performed as a team player. Earning the recognition of his peers would be essential to success in the army because despite the ever-present competition between them, officers equally value selflessness. A powerful sense of camaraderie exists between officers, and he wanted to be seen as a full member of the brotherhood.

He and Holly were fortunate to spend their first four years of active service together at one of the most desirable posts in the army, Vicenza, Italy. When time permitted, they traveled together throughout Italy, Austria, Switzerland, and Germany. But most of the time while Holly stayed busy contributing to activities on the installation like tutoring soldiers seeking their equivalency diplomas, Petraeus threw himself into the hardworking life of a lieutenant in the parachute infantry. He would serve as a platoon leader in C Company, and then later as the S4, or logistics officer for the battalion, and also the S1, or personnel officer on the battalion staff. Most days began with several hours of physical training, followed by marksmanship, small unit drills, and maintenance. Petraeus was always out front, whatever the event. He led his troops to a postchampionship in skiing and racquet ball, and he placed second in cross-country. He earned the Expert Infantryman Badge, or EIB, taking first in the road-march evaluation, and his platoon earned top ranking too. Often he was away on exercises, many of which included airborne drops with the forces of other countries in NATO. He participated in training all over Europe, as widely afield as Scotland, Germany, Italy, and Belgium, earning British, French, and Turkish jump wings along the way.

One such exercise in 1976 would prove to have a lasting influence on the still impressionable officer. That year, he and several dozen troopers from his unit journeyed to France to conduct joint training there. More than a week into the exercise, the combined team performed a difficult parachute insertion onto a high hilltop, followed by a long foot march to a country inn. Whereas in the American army this would probably lead to U.S. soldiers breaking into their cold rations and then finding a spot to sleep on the packed earth, the French hosted Petraeus and his fellow soldiers to an enjoyable dinner complete with well-dressed wait staff. It was one of his first exposures to a different style of military culture.

During this exercise, he also noted a large portrait of the famous French army officer General Marcel Bigeard hanging in a regimental mess. Bigeard had fought for Free France during World War II, and then after the war in Indochina where he valiantly commanded a colonial parachute battalion with great distinction before being taken prisoner at the battle of Dien Bien Phu. He went on to serve Algeria in the 1950s and became a leading proponent of counterinsurgency tactics. Both Bigeard and counterinsurgency as a form of war interested Petraeus, and he began studying both. He studiously read about Bigeard's career and devoured Bernard Falls's books *Hell in a Very Small Place* and *Street Without Joy,* accounts of the history of France's fight to retain Indochina, as well as the classic novel *The Centurions,* by Jean Lartéguy, a novel in which one of the characters is a composite of Bigeard and others. These early investigations made a lasting impression on Petraeus. He marveled at Bigeard's heroics in three wars as a tough, accomplished paratrooper and the kind of thinking leader he no doubt wondered if he could emulate. In 1976 General Knowlton, then serving at NATO headquarters, gave Petraeus a Christmas present that he would cherish and refer to often in the coming years—an autographed picture of Bigeard (with whom he would later correspond as a four-star general).

In July 1979, with a promotion to captain in hand from the previous summer, Petraeus received orders for his next assignment, Fort Stewart, Georgia, the home of the 24th Infantry Division, known by its troopers as the Victory Division. Before he arrived, Petraeus paved his way by writing a letter to Colonel James Shelton, the commander of the 2d Brigade. In the letter, Petraeus asked for the privilege of commanding a rifle company. To support his case, Petraeus noted many of his accomplishments: graduating near the top of his West Point class, honors at the Infantry Basic Course and Ranger School, and sterling performance as a lieutenant in Italy. While it was not unusual for a junior officer to petition for command, Petraeus's letter was particularly confident. But since good officers were always in demand, and if nothing else, Petraeus was demonstrating a sense of boldness, Shelton directed his staff to ensure Petraeus made it to the brigade and was not picked off by any other headquarters. There was always a place for a new lieutenant in the brigade's operations shop. It would be the ideal place to test Petraeus to see if he understood how to plan and organize infantry training exercises. If Petraeus measured up, he'd get the rifle company he sought; if not, there was still plenty of work to be done on the staff.

Fort Stewart, set amid an expansive swath of pine forests about 40 miles southwest of Savannah, was not a highly sought destination, and its predictable rhythms reflected coastal Georgia's deliberate pace of life. When Petraeus and Holly pulled onto the post in their yellow corvette, the installation looked much as it did during the World War II years when it was a major antiaircraft artillery training center for the army. One of the largest posts east of the Mississippi River, it contained nearly 300,000 acres of scrub and swamp. The 24th Division was housed mostly in wooden barracks that had been scheduled to be torn down years before but were still in use because the army lacked the money to replace them.

While not evident to most of the American public, the 24th, like many of its sister divisions, simply wasn't ready for war. The army had been making strides to become a more professional and capable force since it returned from Vietnam earlier in the decade. But the change to an all-volunteer force was difficult. Drugs and indiscipline had permeated the ranks in the late 1960s and 1970s, and it was taking time to root out the troublemakers while simultaneously teaching a new generation of noncommissioned officers how to lead and how to train. At the same time, the army was reorganizing itself and adopting new doctrines that addressed how and where it expected to fight, even as the United States faced increasingly menacing threats overseas.

In November 1979, just several months after Petraeus's arrival at Fort Stewart, radical Islamists seized the American embassy in Tehran, Iran, prompting an international crisis. Soon thereafter, the Soviet Union invaded Afghanistan. These events prompted the United States to examine the readiness of its military forces. The army's leadership in Washington realized that the United States had no sizeable ground force in the Middle East and scant ability to deploy one there if the nation's oil fields near the Persian Gulf were threatened. Nor was there much ability to support an allied state in the region, nor to even evacuate U.S. citizens in the event that they were in danger. It was a period when American security suddenly seemed vulnerable around the world.

Soviet power seemed expansive and growing to the point that it might soon be strong enough to overwhelm U.S. forces in Europe, which had been stripped bare during the Vietnam years. The 1973 Arab oil embargo reinforced calls for a peace dividend to shore up the federal budget, which wasn't the last time that the political class turned a blind eye to strategic imperatives in favor of domestic political momentum. At the same time, the needs of America's all-volunteer armed forces meant that spending priorities were focused on recruitment and retention and away from equipment and readiness. Hence the U.S. approach in the 1970s was to accept a high level of risk, but this was not sustainable, and soon events overseas began to crowd U.S. defense priorities at a time when the very nature of ground combat seemed to be changing.

The Yom Kippur War, fought in October 1973, appeared to point to the future. In that conflict, heavy fighting erupted when Egyptian and Syrian forces conducted a surprise attack on Israel. The combat featured an abundance of antitank weapons, including rocket-propelled grenades and guided missiles. Quickly regrouping, the Israeli army counterattacked aggressively, ultimately regaining the ground they had lost in the opening hours of the war and inflicting heavy casualties on their Arab opponents. The war demonstrated that heavy armored formations could move with alacrity and great lethality when commanded decisively. It also showed the growing importance of missiles and rocket-propulsion technologies for ground combat. It was a sharp and violent war, leading military thinkers to conclude that armies must be trained and ready at the onset of conflict. Arab and Israeli forces together lost more tanks in the space of two weeks than the entire U.S. Army possessed in Europe.

It was in this context that President Jimmy Carter announced the establishment of a rapid deployment force, consisting of air, ground, and naval forces that would be able to deploy and fight in the Middle East on short notice. The 24th Division, newly converted to a mechanized force, meaning it was to receive new trucks, armored personnel carriers, and tanks to give it much greater mobility and firepower, was to be a part of this new force. And it was slated to deploy, if called upon, in the Middle East. But it wasn't ready yet. As General Edward Meyer, the army chief of staff told President Carter the same month the embassy was taken over in Iran, "Mr. President, basically what we have is a hollow Army."[1] This short, accurate assessment would prove to be a bumper sticker describing

the low state of readiness of the army, a condition that Petraeus's generation of officers would spend their professional lives working to correct.

Petraeus's time at Fort Stewart, as well as his later career, would be
profoundly affected by these issues, but for the moment, Petraeus didn't
aim to remain in the 24th. He had plans for higher-profile duty with the
ranger battalion stationed there. As elite formations, the ranger units
were the most highly trained forces and possessed the best equipment.
He knew that the rangers offered him the best opportunity to be challenged by other high-performing soldiers. As always, he wanted to test
himself against the best the army had. But in the meantime, he needed
to learn his new duties in the 24th. He would need to do well there if he
hoped to move across post to the ranger battalion.

In characteristic fashion, he leapt vigorously into his responsibilities,
quickly demonstrating that he was a hard worker and a quick study. His
chain of command soon rewarded him with company command, meaning he was directly responsible for more than a hundred soldiers. Company command is a significant milestone in the life of junior officers,
and performance as a commanding officer goes far toward establishing
oneself in the profession. He faced an immediate challenge though. As
a mechanized division, his unit relied upon vehicles to transport them
and heavier weapon systems than he had experienced in the airborne
infantry in Italy. To ensure that he learned how to maintain all of the
new equipment, and to be able to supervise his mechanics, Petraeus
began spending large amounts of time in the unit motor pool and garage
areas where the vehicles were stored. Always a stickler for adherence to
published standards, and never reluctant to be the center of attention,
Petraeus placed himself in the middle of the action. With a megaphone
in one hand and an opened maintenance manual in the other, he would
recite the individual maintenance tasks, one by one. From filters to
belts to transmission work, he stayed there for hours on end, drilling the
mechanics, who would have much preferred to fix things in their own
way. But over time, the vehicles in Petraeus's unit began showing improved readiness rates, and he earned the grudging respect of the wrench
turners. They may not have loved Petraeus for the way he dictated the
standards to them, but they couldn't argue with the results either. As
Petraeus noted much later, "If you want to show seriousness of purpose,
you personally commit to it."[2]

In this as in nearly every aspect of his duties, Petraeus demonstrated nearly inexhaustible energy. Many days he would run the two miles from his house to the unit headquarters and then lead his company on their full range of exercises, including a three- to five-mile run before returning home to shower. He got along well with his fellow commanders, and his lieutenants admired him deeply. A few of his peers thought that he tried too hard by turning nearly everything into competitions, but in Petraeus's view, competition was a way of measuring himself and his unit. He thought that the only way to achieve excellence was to push hard. He even created competition where most would not imagine that any existed. On one occasion, he read in a local newspaper that three of the rangers had run as a team between Savannah and Fort Stewart, setting a new record in the process. So Petraeus captained a team of his own and outpaced the rangers' time by a fair margin. It was classic Petraeus. A similar instance of his desire to stand out came while he was the coach of a company basketball team. He promised his team that he would bring a four-star general to watch them if they made it to the postchampionship game. While one can wonder if this was really motivational for the soldiers, Petraeus genuinely thought so. Thus, when the team did make it to the championship, Petraeus coordinated a visit by General Knowlton. Petraeus's strategy must have worked, because he and his team won the game.

The next day, Petraeus accomplished a more significant milestone. The Expert Infantryman Badge, or EIB, which Petraeus had earned for himself as a lieutenant, is a prestigious badge that denotes a soldier's mastery of critical infantry skills and is difficult to attain because it is carefully graded by impartial judges. While most company commanders viewed the EIB as nice to have but not a priority, Petraeus wanted as many of his soldiers to earn the EIB as possible, so he made it a central aspect of his company's training regimen. He drove his men through a detailed and rigorous program as they prepared for the evaluation. From weapons qualification to land navigation to first aid, Petraeus and his leadership worked and worked to improve their proficiency. Ultimately, fully 65 percent of Petraeus's company earned the EIB, which meant that his company could fly the Expert Infantry Company Streamer, the only company in the division to earn such a right. It was a remarkable feat that established Petraeus's reputation at Fort Stewart as a leader who got results. While this also caused some of the other officers on post to criticize Petraeus for taking too much attention, they couldn't dispute his success. Colonel Shelton heard the murmuring but valued officers who set high standards and led their troops to meet them. When the job of battalion operations officer, or S3, became vacant in one of the battalions within the brigade soon after, a position normally occupied by a major, Shelton put Petraeus in the position. Petraeus was quite junior for the duty, and only 10 months into his company command, but he agreed to the transition.

When word got out that Petraeus was to be promoted over officers ahead of him in the queue, Major General James Cochran objected. Shelton stood his ground, arguing that Petraeus may have been junior in years and experience, but that he was the best qualified and deserved a shot. Cochran retreated, and Petraeus found himself again with the opportunity to demonstrate his abilities. As the S3, one of the three most senior positions in the battalion (the executive officer is a major, and the battalion commander is a lieutenant colonel), responsible for planning and supervising the unit's operations, whether that be a training exercise or if the unit is deployed, in combat, Petraeus shined. His organizational and communication abilities came into play, and soon he reorganized the other officers under his supervision to create better, more realistic training events. He was an expert writer and drafted effective, clear orders for the unit. The other captains did their utmost to keep up with him, but matching Petraeus's energy wasn't always easy. For Petraeus, it wasn't personal. He just didn't have much patience with those who couldn't match his drive.

An attribute that his bosses liked the most was that Petraeus could marshal a variety of resources available to the unit and direct them to a common purpose. In one instance, he orchestrated a live-fire exercise, a high-profile training event that involved ground vehicles such as tanks and personnel carriers moving and firing while overhead helicopters launched rockets and attacked targets, all using live ammunition. Such exercises, while having real benefit for the participating troops, were as much spectacle for families, friends, and senior officers from around post who gathered to watch from a designated viewing area. When complete, Petraeus beamed with pride at what he had directed. It had indeed been a show, even if it had cost a hefty share of the battalion's yearly ammunition budget. But Petraeus wasn't worried about that aspect. He knew that he could soon gain more ammunition by borrowing from other units that were not going to use their allocations. Once again, Petraeus's aggressiveness paid off in a very visible way.

Petraeus's year as the S3 passed quickly, and in May 1981, the 24th Division received a new commander, Major General John Galvin. He soon learned about the exceptional officer serving as operations officer in the 2d Brigade and hired Petraeus to be his aide-de-camp. The position of an aide is a challenging one. Aides take on the traditional role of a personal assistant who supervises schedules, monitors private correspondence, and attends to whatever particular needs a commanding general may have. Only those officers who possess the military bearing and ability to work independently are selected. Sometimes, aides are also employed to offer candid advice, and it was this latter role that Galvin sought Petraeus to perform. Galvin instructed his new aide, "It's my job to run the division, and it's your job to help me expand my impact and to critique me."[3] He was looking for someone in whom he could place his confidence and who could serve as an additional observer of people and events in the division. He and Petraeus quickly became close and formed an effective partnership.

A willful, quietly proud, and deeply intellectual man who had begun his career as an enlisted soldier before graduating from West Point in 1954, Galvin was a unique, full character. He had served two distinguished tours in Vietnam and had found trouble with his superiors for objecting to the American practice of counting enemy fatalities, known as the *body count,* as a way of measuring success. In addition to his prowess on the battlefield, Galvin demonstrated a lifelong commitment to learning, earning a master's degree at Columbia University en route to an assignment at the academy's Department of English. There he taught literature and developed a deep appreciation for the army's role as a reforming agent in American society, developing ideas that were sometimes unconventional by the mainstream force. He wrote often in his spare time and was a true soldier-scholar, which appealed to Petraeus.

Once in command, Galvin moved aggressively to make the 24th capable of fulfilling its rapid deployment role. He created and supervised up-to-date training and maintenance programs that dramatically improved unit combat readiness of the division. Vehicles and equipment were painted desert tan, exercises based on Middle Eastern deployment scenarios were initiated, and leader development was taken seriously. Overall, the pace picked up at Fort Stewart, a transformation Petraeus watched from a privileged perch.

As Petraeus took fondly to his boss, so Galvin admired Petraeus. He appreciated the way that Petraeus kept his schedule humming efficiently and was thankful that Petraeus developed a fine sense for the daily priorities of the command. He realized right away that Petraeus could be useful to him as a source for objective assessments, even of his own performance as the commanding general.

Of course, Petraeus's nearness to his boss did lead to some tension between Petraeus and other members of the general's personal staff. The division chief of staff, a colonel several grades senior to Petraeus, reprimanded the aggressive aide several times for being what the chief thought was too brash. Petraeus took it in stride. Like all aides, he understood that he walked a fine line between serving the general and meeting his specific requirements while at the same time fitting in with the rest of the staff. If he was chewed out once in awhile along the way, well that was just the cost of doing business.

The longer Galvin and Petraeus served together, the closer they became. In the spring of 1982, while Galvin sat on a several-week promotion board in Washington, Petraeus seized the opportunity to attend Air Assault School at Fort Campbell, Kentucky—billed as the "ten toughest days in the Army." Petraeus breezed through, finishing as the Distinguished Honor Graduate and the road-march champion. That same year, elements of the division traveled to Fort Irwin, California, the home of the army's National Training Center. The NTC, as it is known, had recently opened and was the army's premier force-on-force maneuver area. Its origins lay in the army's studies of battle experiences in World War II, Korea, and Vietnam. What was learned was that U.S. ground forces suffered very high casualties in their first battles—and the army rarely won its initial contests, no matter who the enemy or the circumstances. There was thus a clear need to train army forces in peacetime in a way that would save blood during wartime. The navy had conducted a similar kind of evaluation and had noted that a similarly steep learning curve had existed in the first years of air-to-air combat in Vietnam. To address this, the navy had in 1969 instituted a training program that would be popularized in American culture in the 1986 movie *Top Gun*.

The army's version at NTC pitted against an opposing force, or *OpFor*, consisting of U.S. troops dressed and equipped to look and act like Warsaw Pact and Soviet troops. Each side donned Multiple Integrated Laser Engagement System (MILES) harnesses that allowed hits to be recorded by computer. The OpFor was very good. They trained against U.S. (or *BlueFor*) units for much of the year, and they knew how to maneuver and fight over the NTC's rugged desert landscape using Eastern bloc tactics. The American army, however, had not waged war using large formations of tanks and mechanized infantry for decades, and the search for new ways of fighting, and training to fight, were yet underway.

The army's official doctrine, termed *active defense*, was contained in the 1976 version of its capstone doctrinal publication, Field Manual 100-5, *Operations*. This publication was the army's formal statement that described how army units move and fight on the battlefield. It tried to accommodate the many political and financial constraints of the decade, but few were satisfied with it. The manual restricted army forces to a role of limited maneuver because it assumed that NATO would not allow the relinquishment of any territory. Thus, U.S. forces were supposed to remain on the defensive in relatively static positions, fighting Warsaw Pact troops in place as they attacked. Fortunately, a new doctrine was emerging. AirLand Battle, which was formally adopted in the 1982 version of FM 100-5, was a revolutionary vision of warfare that was unlike anything the army had attempted prior. It was these tenets that the 24th was trying to carry out at Fort Irwin but struggling to implement.

Developed beginning in the late 1970s, AirLand Battle was a doctrine that looked at a broad theater of warfare in its entirety. It argued that U.S. forces, stuck in largely static positions, would likely be defeated. Even if U.S. troops won the first battle, follow-on Soviet echelons would overrun U.S. and NATO troops. To counter such an outcome, AirLand Battle posed that army assets such as long-range rockets, attack helicopters, and tactical air force fighters would attack deep enemy targets. Army forces would also be released to fully maneuver in depth to their best advantage. A further benefit was that AirLand Battle was not restricted to the European theater. It applied to the still unstable Korean Peninsula, and relevant to Galvin's 24th, it could be used in the Middle

East. It was a challenging way of war fighting because it required subordinate leaders to make timely and effective decisions, a talent not enough junior officers yet possessed. During most of the two-week exercise, the OpFor outperformed the 24th. Galvin's men showed real improvement, but it was also clear that a great deal of work remained before the division was truly war ready. Petraeus watched it all, taking careful notes of the division's shortcomings.

While watching the division's troops train hard for combat from his perch as the aide-de-camp, he thought often about the fact that it was nearly time for him to move on to another assignment. Galvin had realized early on that Petraeus was worth investing in, and so he had made sure to spend time personally teaching his eager captain. Petraeus had always been devoted to the study of leadership, yet after several years of active duty, he still found it difficult to admit when he made a mistake. Galvin encouraged him to be more flexible, both with himself and with others. He told Petraeus that to really attain success he would have to think beyond the regimented culture of the infantry branch. Being in top physical condition and maxing training exercises was a core requirement, but there was much more that leaders who truly aspired to success must do. Galvin emphasized the power of history as an instructive tool to examine problems in the search for novel solutions. He stressed to Petraeus that he must think about how armies relate to the societies that support them, and what the next war the army is asked to fight may look like. Importantly, he encouraged Petraeus to consider attending graduate school. Exposing Petraeus to civilian students and professors, many who no doubt would possess very different ideas than did Petraeus with his military education and training, would do wonders, Galvin knew.

With his time coming to an end at Fort Stewart and a rotation to another assignment upcoming, Petraeus's earlier ambition to join the Rangers at Fort Stewart seemed to approach. Then, to his surprise, Petraeus and eight other captains were selected two years early to attend the Command and General Staff School (CGSC), at Fort Leavenworth, Kansas.

Situated astride a high bluff on the western bank of the Missouri River about 25 miles from downtown Kansas City, the post boasts a long history. The oldest continuously active army post west of the Mississippi

River, it began in 1827 as a frontier outpost protecting the westward migration of wagon trains and safeguarding settlements along the Indian frontier. CGSC was founded in 1883 and since its establishment had served as an educational center for midgrade army officers. It reached its zenith during the early 20th century when the generals who would lead the American war effort during World War II passed through, such as Dwight D. Eisenhower, Omar N. Bradley, and George S. Patton. By the 1980s, although much faded from its heyday and by then on a trajectory that would see its central role in the education of officers largely ended due to broadening learning experiences available at other schools, it was still a critical stop for any officer who wanted to be advanced to the ranks of colonel and beyond. Most of the students were newly promoted majors, with only the top 50 percent of any year group of officers attending, but Petraeus was selected while still a midgrade captain, an experiment the army discontinued soon thereafter.

Petraeus, the youngest officer in the course, was housed alongside his fellow captains separately from the main body of officers, increasing the sense of intimidation felt by some of his peers. But Petraeus shook off any initial hesitation and worked hard to excel. He saw his junior rank as just another motivation to test himself against officers who had several years' more experience than he had. His efforts paid off at the end of the school year when in May he learned that he would be the top graduate and thus the George C. Marshall Award winner, popularly known as the holder of the white briefcase and a distinction that officers remembered and noted throughout their careers. Petraeus was the last of two captains to earn this distinction (the other was Wesley Clark, who would retire as a four-star general in 2000).

During his year at Leavenworth, Petraeus considered General Galvin's guidance that civilian graduate school was the path to deeper understanding about the army and the route to take to becoming a better leader. But Petraeus knew that the path to graduate school also carried professional risks. The conventional wisdom of the majority of senior officers was that majors needed to stay close to soldiers. Spending time in a civilian college was thought at best an unfortunate distraction, and at worst an attempt to avoid the real army by choosing a comfortable life for a few years. Nonetheless, Petraeus was confident in himself, and during his year at Leavenworth, he had thought deeply about the army.

The prospects of further intellectual studies intrigued him. With the examples of soldier-scholars Knowlton and Galvin in mind, he decided to buck the professional trend and attend Princeton University on the way to an assignment teaching in the Social Sciences Department back at West Point. It was a momentous decision, and one that would influence the rest of his life.

NOTES

1. James Kitfield, *Prodigal Soldiers*, Association of the United States Army Institute of Land Warfare Series (Washington, DC: Potomac Books, 1997), 199.

2. Cloud and Jaffe, *The Fourth Star*, 38.

3. Ibid., 42.

Chapter 4

EXPANDING HORIZONS: THE YOUNG SCHOLAR-LEADER

In the autumn of 1984, Holly and Petraeus packed their household and with newly arrived Anne, their first child, moved to New Jersey. Petraeus was enrolled in Princeton University's graduate program of the Woodrow Wilson School of Public and International Affairs. They lived near the campus in a small townhome and fashioned for themselves a lifestyle that was distinctly different from the more regimented and fishbowl-like routines that were the norm on military installations. But they were no less busy as Petraeus threw himself into the curriculum as if it were a military opponent. He was determined to master this new challenge and soon decided that he would not only pursue his master's degree but also take on the extra coursework and exams that would allow him to depart Princeton in two years on the path to earning a doctoral degree.

Whereas life at West Point as a cadet had been filled with order and regulation, the atmosphere at Princeton was nearly the opposite: students had enormous leeway about how they filled their days. Petraeus knew that despite the far-reaching contrasts in style, each was specifically adopted to further the pursuit of knowledge, and each strived for excellence and to be the very best institution of its kind. West Point had taught him the value of self-discipline and had rewarded the ability to perform assignments quickly, moving from one task to another to make it through the prodigious workload thrown at cadets. The academic program at the academy was like a series of sprints, and cadets who could maintain a fast pace earned high marks. Princeton both offered and rewarded a different kind of intellectual pursuit. Petraeus's new professors emphasized deep and careful introspection. They insisted that he assemble the arguments of his papers carefully and that he examine volume after volume of history.

As many military officers who first delve into civilian academia find, it proved to be a daunting undertaking. A professor noted on one of his papers his first year that, "Though the paper is reasonably well-written and has some merit, it is relatively simplistic and I am left feeling that the whole is less than the sum of the parts."[1] Petraeus was dismayed to see a B on another paper. And on a microeconomics exam, he even received a D, an extraordinarily humbling moment. Accustomed to being ahead of his peers—from star man at West Point to general's aide to the top grad at Leavenworth—Petraeus found that he needed to regroup and redouble his efforts in this new environment. He rebounded to finish his first year by earning academic distinction, the equivalent of honors, as he scored six As and two A-minuses. Thus, right away Princeton became a challenging and invigorating experience that would move him out of his intellectual comfort zone, but one that he could master.

Taking advantage of the opportunity to write a new seminar paper, he decided to delve into the issues that he had seen being debated during his previous tours. In Italy, his exercises with French paratroopers had introduced him to the tradition of colonial conflicts as exemplified by General Bigeard. There he had learned about the need for great powers to wage war for specific national interests short of a total war effort. Then with General Galvin and the 24th Division at Fort Stewart, he had witnessed the vast transformation underway in how the army was preparing to fight on future battlefields. So for his paper topic, a determined Petraeus chose to look at the ways the Vietnam War had influenced the presidential administrations of Nixon, Ford, and Carter as they employed, or contemplated the employment of, U.S. forces. When Zbigniew Brzezinski, the former national security advisor to President Carter, visited Princeton, Petraeus showed his typical initiative by volunteering to escort him all the way to Washington so that he could use the traveling time to informally conduct an interview. When he earned an A-plus on the paper, Petraeus decided to continue this line of inquiry for his doctoral work. Now committed to a topic and a new goal, he aggressively set out during the rest of his academic sojourn to complete the necessary course-work. He would have to complete the dissertation itself during his follow-on tour of duty.

During the summer between his first and second years, Petraeus worked for then colonel Wesley Clark and alongside fellow captain John Abizaid in Army Chief of Staff General John Wickham's Army Studies Group. This team of high-flying officers helped the chief sharpen army programs by writing critical and analytical essays, some of which were published in ARMY magazine on critical topics.

Looking back on his time at Princeton, Petraeus would credit the uni-versity with imparting to him an intellectual agility and maturity that he had not gained from military service. Observing civilian academia showed that the brightest minds in other disciplines attacked problems and found solutions just as effectively as did military officers, but often in very different ways. He learned to write and communicate with greater polish and authority and became comfortable with the give-and-take of academic debate. Whereas the military was a strictly hierarchical orga-nization with orders and direction flowing from the top down, the uni-versity was organized differently. Petraeus could see the value of a more level exchange of information as professors and students challenged one another with ideas. The faculty certainly provided direction, but stu-dents were empowered to speak up and offer informed and contrasting viewpoints. It was much more tumultuous, provocative, and in many ways both uncomfortable and inspiring. Furthermore, as a military officer on an elite campus and the only army officer in the Woodrow Wilson School that year, he found himself to be a distinct minority.

In many classes, he had to vigorously defend his positions regarding national security and foreign policy. He found out that there were strongly held positions on nearly all matters of strategy and politics. Up to this point, he and his army peers had debated many details about military programs and priorities but could find agreement that a strong national defense was warranted. Now, even consensus on the foundational points of American government seemed lacking among his civilian classmates, and all assumptions were up for debate. Previously, he had taken West

Point's motto of Duty, Honor, Country for granted and assumed that all, or nearly all, Americans shared the same convictions. At Princeton, there were some who defined patriotism in ways that seemed at odds with the academy's vision for the nation. It amounted to an invigorating period of development that reframed and strengthened Petraeus's intellectual approach. His natural penchant for asking questions was stimulated even further, and he gained better tools of research and mental agility, and even a kind of intellectual depth that made him even tougher.

When in the spring of 1985 he was awarded his master's degree in public and international affairs, he once again packed up his household. This time, they were headed back to a place they had already been, West Point. However, this time Petraeus was going to serve on the faculty of one of the most influential organizations not only at the academy but in the army itself, the Department of Social Sciences.

NOTE

1. Cloud and Jaffe, *The Fourth Star*, 61.

Chapter 5

BACK TO USMA: DUTY IN THE DEPARTMENT OF SOCIAL SCIENCES

West Point's primary mission is to teach, educate, train, and inspire cadets to become army officers and to serve the nation. However, it also bears a second, nearly as important responsibility that is largely overlooked—the education and training of its faculty, the bulk of whom are senior captains and majors who return to the field-army after their tour at the academy as instructors, armed with new thinking and fresh ideas. However, the cultural bias in the army has always been toward decision and action, rather than introspection and discussion. Officers who seek assignment as instructors frequently meet discouragement from more senior leaders, especially in the combat arms branches, who feel that duty close to operational units is better preparation for higher rank. So when Petraeus reported to Sosh, as the Department of Social Sciences is most frequently known, he knew that he was joining a special group of officers, each with keen academic backgrounds who had chosen to come to the department in the face of a fair degree of professional adversity. Sosh department alumni make a distinguished roster of national leaders, both past and present. Petraeus was eager to enter the mix.

The department's primary charter was to teach politics, government, economics, and international relations courses to cadets. All second-year cadets (the yearlings) were introduced to the department's instructors through the core economics class, and nearly all cadets took a variety of foreign policy and government classes during their years as upperclassmen. It was located, along with a number of other teaching departments, deep within the massive Thayer Hall, the former riding hall, which looms like a medieval fortress on a cliff overlooking the Hudson. Often, especially in winter, officers would report in the early morning darkness to labor within Thayer's gray walls, not emerging until after nightfall, never once having seen daylight that day.

As soon as Petraeus settled into West Point in the summer of 1985, he resumed work on his dissertation, "The American Military and the Lessons of Vietnam: A Study of Military Influence and the Use of Force in the Post-Vietnam Era." The army's experience in Vietnam had been wrenching, and in its wake, significant reforms were underway that were the subject of much debate at West Point. There was much consternation about the war's results. Its unpopularity at home coupled with battlefield action in which the army demonstrated conventional prowess but could not link its tactical victories with a broader political and strategic campaign continued to perplex. Officers staked out positions whether the disconnect was due more to civilian political mistakes or errors and miscommunications by its own leadership. This was the issue that Petraeus had begun to explore at graduate school and now developed more fully.

In his 328-page thesis, many of the ideas that would later come to fruition as he led the U.S. efforts in Iraq and Afghanistan can be seen. Regarding the lessons of history about war, he noted,

> Historical analogies are particularly compelling during crises, when the tendency to supplement incomplete information with past experiences is especially marked . . . the legacy of Vietnam is unlikely to soon recede as an important influence on America's senior military.[1]

In terms of the army's experience in Southeast Asia, he observed that,

> Vietnam was an extremely painful reminder that when it comes to intervention, time and patience are not American virtues in abundant supply. Vietnam cost the military dearly. It left America's

military leaders confounded, dismayed, and discouraged. . . . While the psychic scars of the war may be deepest among the Army and Marine Corps leadership, however, the senior leaders of all the services share a similar reaction to Vietnam. There is no desire among any of them to repeat the experience.[2]

He also commented with great insight, that war is political in nature, and the view from the battlefield and the view from Washington must both be considered by a commander: "The military also took from Vietnam (and the concomitant activities in the Pentagon) a heightened awareness that civilian officials are responsive to influences other than the objective conditions on the battlefield."[3] It was a lesson that he absorbed, and one that he would employ himself, many times. Looking ahead, Petraeus noted that the task for his generation of officers was to find a better way. As he wrote, "For the military, in short, the debate over how and when to commit American troops abroad has become a debate over how to avoid, at all costs, another Vietnam."[4]

Petraeus's investigation came at a rich time for retrospection because much of what he wrote about in his paper derived from his direct experiences as a young officer. When the army departed Vietnam, it did eagerly put the many traumas of that war in the rearview mirror. As an institution, the army looked nearly exclusively at the looming conventional war threats in Europe, Korea, and the Middle East for opponents against whom to model training and doctrine. Changes in the army had picked up speed in the late 1970s as it completely reformed its manpower policies and doctrine and developed key weapon systems. These changes, like those Petraeus had been a part of at Fort Stewart and the 24th Division, would ultimately result in an army that stared down the Soviet and Warsaw Pact troops in Europe and devastated Saddam Hussein's invading army in Kuwait during the 1991 Persian Gulf War, but that still lay in the future, and such feats seemed far away.

Most of the army's senior leadership felt comfortable looking ahead with confidence while looking back at Vietnam with care. It had been a searing experience for most soldiers, and emotions were still raw. Petraeus commented on this in his paper: "The legacy of Vietnam is unlikely to soon recede as an important influence on America's senior military. The frustrations of Vietnam are too deeply etched in the minds of those who now the [sic] lead the services and combatant commands."[5] Nonetheless, at West Point, Vietnam and its consequences lingered in the conversation. A small but prolific group of officers persisted to examine Vietnam to better understand its outcome. Petraeus framed the issue: "For the military, in short, the debate over how and when to commit American troops abroad has become a debate over how to avoid, at all costs, another Vietnam."[6]

In the summer of 1985, the Sosh department hosted a conference in recognition of North Vietnam's triumph over America's former ally, South Vietnam. The army's instinctive response to Vietnam was to heap blame on a feckless political class who denied military leaders the resources necessary to launch and win the massive assaults against North Vietnamese targets that uniformed commanders often advocated. The published literature that had arisen during the intervening years went in two different directions to describe Vietnam. On the one hand, some scribes looked at the conflict in strategic terms, locating America's failures there as a matter of insufficient national will. Others found refuge by focusing on the army's many victories at the unit level. Petraeus and his fellow Sosh professors found neither description of the army in Vietnam to be satisfying and began asking different questions. While Petraeus noted that "nothing succeeds with the American public like success, the military realize; the sooner the mission is accomplished, the better," he questioned whether the army was really preparing for the full range of conflicts that could be on the horizon.[7]

Petraeus wasn't critical of the dedication the army was placing against conventional combat; he had seen how much progress was being made while on exercises at the National Training Center and at Fort Stewart. But he did regard its near-exclusive focus on this kind of high intensity war to be a mistake. He argued that the army must also prepare to fight irregular wars. This was against the grain of thinking in the Pentagon. It would be a tough proposition to change the culture of the army to develop a counterinsurgency mentality. Petraeus cited the comment of an officer that summed up the army's view: "The U.S. Army does not have the mind-set for combat operations where the key terrain is the mind, not the high ground. We do not take the time to understand the nature of the society in which we are fighting, the government we are supporting, or the enemy we are fighting."[8]

This last point particularly troubled Petraeus. From his studies at Princeton and long conversations with his father-in-law, General Knowlton, and his mentor, General Galvin, each of whom had served in Vietnam, Petraeus believed the army must be more flexible. He knew it was an uphill argument because, as he wrote: "The military want to avoid what former Army Chief of Staff Edward C. Meyer termed the Vietnam mistake of 'putting soldiers out at the end of a string' without the full support of the American people. Since time is crucial, furthermore, sufficient force must be used at the outset to ensure that the conflict can be resolved before the American people withdraw their support for it."[9]

Petraeus continued to write. He did not feel that his dissertation was ready to be published, but in the Autumn 1986 issue of the military journal *Parameters,* he authored an article, "Lessons of History and Lessons of Vietnam." In it he echoed the themes he had been thinking about and researching. Petraeus extolled the virtue of looking to the past for strategic solutions, while noting that in the case of Vietnam, it could sometimes hamstring leaders: "In short, rather than preparing to fight the last war, as generals and admirals are often accused of doing, contemporary military leaders seem far more inclined to avoid any involvement overseas that could become another Vietnam." He added that, "Vietnam also increased the military inclination toward the 'all or nothing' type of advice." As he summarized, "There is a conviction that when it comes to the use of force, America should either bite the bullet or duck, but not nibble."[10] In other words, in Vietnam the army wound up fighting the war it wanted to fight rather than the one it needed to fight. It could not afford to make that mistake again. The army must take some of the blame for what happened in Vietnam and then move ahead to recognize that small wars were an unavoidable part of the security landscape. This wouldn't be easy because "the senior military is thus in a dilemma. The lessons taken from Vietnam would indicate that, in general, involvement in a counterinsurgency should be avoided. But prudent preparation for a likely contingency . . . lead the military to recognize that significant emphasis should be given to counterinsurgency forces, equipment, and doctrine."[11]

But even if conflicts were unpopular, the army must be prepared to fight them. As Petraeus counseled, "The military should look beyond critiques of American involvement in Vietnam that focus exclusively on alternative conventional military strategies that might have been pursued.[12]" It could not avoid regional contests simply because of the risk that one could escalate. The next time it found itself in a guerrilla war, it could not afford to alienate the local populace. It must possess war-fighting capabilities across the spectrum so it could effectively tie its military tactics with broader operational and even strategic campaigns to protect the population and direct military power against engaged enemies, not the innocent bystanders. Petraeus's conclusion was that at the end of the day, Vietnam was an important case study, but contemporary events warranted study as well: "History in general, and the American experience in Vietnam in particular, have much to teach us, but both must be used with discretion and neither should be pushed too far."[13]

An article largely written by Petraeus but appearing under General Galvin's name in a subsequent issue of *Parameters* reinforced these arguments. The essay was structured around a talk that Galvin had recently delivered on counterinsurgency where he said, "There are many indicators that we are moving into a world in which subversive activities, civil disturbances, guerrilla warfare, and low-level violence will grow and multiply." He added, "Warfare is thus no longer fought simply by the military. It now encompasses entire populations, large or small."[14] It was an idea that he and Petraeus had often bantered about. Soon the two were reunited and had the chance to once again look at the issues of small wars firsthand together. During the summer between his first and second years of teaching, Petraeus traveled to the headquarters of U.S. Southern Command in the Panama Canal Zone, where General Galvin was then commanding.

Being away from West Point reminded Petraeus of the challenges facing the United States. Conflict in Central America and Africa were on the rise and seemed to increasingly be threatening regional stability. The cold war was at its height, and America's ability to confront Soviet proxies would be a key addition to the U.S. arsenal. In El Salvador, U.S. special operations troops were directly supporting the Salvadoran government by providing intelligence, funds, training, and according to public reports, direct action. Nearby in Nicaragua, America had taken the opposite tack, this time fueling the *contras*, who were insurgents opposing the leftist Sandinista government. In Afghanistan, the CIA was providing arms to Muslim fighters, and in Africa, there seemed to be plentiful opportunities to thwart a variety of Marxist-inspired movements. None of these American efforts were large in scale, but they did generate much public comment, and in the major media centers of New York and Washington, a great deal of opposition.

From his headquarters in Panama, Galvin was responsible for the army's most significant of counterinsurgency operations since Vietnam. The scale was much smaller, as Congress had placed strict ceilings on the commitment. The Reagan administration viewed such limits as more permeable but had nonetheless concurred that it was best to keep the fighting there contained, both in scope and magnitude of U.S. forces involved. American troops were barred from direct combat actions, but were present on the ground as advisors and trainers. Petraeus, just like he had done as an aide-de-camp, attached himself to Galvin's command group as they traveled through the region, including stops in El Salvador, Honduras, and Panama. They observed how army troops prepared to fight in equatorial climes, visiting the 23,000 acres of rain forest at the Jungle Operations Training Center, Fort Sherman, Panama. Petraeus, always eager to be near the front lines, found it an invigorating experience. El Salvador was his first experience of being in a war zone. He could see that the army was indeed engaged in the kinds of operations he had been contemplating.

While most officers taught for three years in the Sosh Department, Petraeus was ready to leave the academy. He was sensitive to the fact that he'd already spent four years on the academic side of the force and wanted to be closer to troops and to burnish his operational credentials by returning to life in the infantry. So when General Galvin, who had been selected to go to Europe in his new role as supreme Allied commander of NATO, offered Petraeus the chance to work as a speechwriter, Petraeus was pleased with the opportunity. Petraeus knew he would be at a four-star headquarters and not in a field unit, but he would be able to work for his mentor in a setting that would allow him to meet people. And it would probably only be for a year. At that point, Petraeus would be due to again serve in an infantry battalion.

Still, such a sudden reassignment was not Petraeus's decision to make. Hence, General Galvin contacted the superintendent to ask for the release of his former aide. This kind of request was not out of the ordinary. It was true that Petraeus enjoyed advantages not possessed by most, but in each case, he had risen to the opportunities presented to him and excelled.

Writing at a feverish pace through the spring, Petraeus excitedly wrapped up his dissertation, graduating with a doctorate in International Relations. In June 1987, he, Holly, Anne, and their second child, Stephen, who had been born the year prior, headed to Europe.

NOTES

1. Rachel Dry, "Petraeus on Vietnam's Legacy" [excerpts from General Petraeus's dissertation], *Washington Post*, January 14, 2007. http://www.washingtonpost.com/wp-dyn/content/article/2007/01/12/AR2007011201955.html.

2. Ibid.

3. Ibid.

4. Ibid.

5. Ibid.

6. Ibid.

7. Ibid.

8. Ibid.

9. Ibid.

10. David H. Petraeus, "Lessons of History and Lessons of Vietnam," *Parameters* 16, no. 3 (1986), 46.

11. Ibid., 49.

12. Ibid., 50.

13. Ibid., 51.

14. John R. Galvin, "Uncomfortable Wars: Toward a New Paradigm," *Parameters* 16, no. 4 (1986), 5.

Chapter 6

FIELD-GRADE YEARS

Petraeus and Holly were pleased to be returning to Europe, their first home together as an army family. This time, however, they began their tour at Supreme Headquarters Allied Powers Europe (SHAPE) in Mons, Belgium. From this perch, Petraeus could clearly observe how coalitions fashion policy. His time in the Sosh department proved to be timely and relevant preparation. As he had taught international relations, economics, and international security issues, not to mention had run the conference "NATO at Forty," he was ready to engage in the kinds of strategy development ongoing at SHAPE. It proved to be a thrilling year. He participated firsthand in the negotiations surrounding the Intermediate Nuclear Forces Agreement, in which General Galvin played a pivotal role, briefing the president and cabinet and testifying before Congress. Petraeus wrote 10 articles for him and dozens of speeches, all the while continuing to think about the military profession on his own as well and to see his articles in print. In 1989, the journal *Armed Forces & Society* published his essay, "Military Influence and the Post-Vietnam Use of Force," which carried forward his reflections.

The late 1980s were the heyday of the post-Vietnam changes in the army, especially in Europe, where the army's premier war-fighting units were deployed. The Reagan administration's investments in key weapon systems, such as the UH-60 Blackhawk (utility and transport helicopter), M1 Abrams tank, the AH-64 Apache (attack helicopter), the Patriot (air defense missile), and the M3 Bradley infantry fighting vehicle were paying tremendous dividends. The training and doctrine revolutions that Petraeus had experienced at Fort Stewart had migrated to Europe. The premier Combat Maneuver Training Center (CMTC) located at Hohenfels, Germany, featured high-quality force-on-force maneuver exercises, and the divisions in Europe were benefiting from assignment of many of the best officers and noncommissioned officers from across the force. It was a popular destination because with the cold war still ongoing, facing the Soviets along the inner-German border was rightly seen as the army's chief mission.

Petraeus only served a year at SHAPE, transferring in the summer of 1988 to Schweinfurt, Germany, to begin a three-year tour with the 3d Infantry Division. The 3ID had been stationed in Europe since 1958 and was a mechanized formation fully benefiting from the army's recent upgrades in equipment, training, and personnel. Petraeus was initially the battalion operations officer for the 2d Battalion, 30th Infantry Regiment, before being transferred to the headquarters of the 1st Brigade, where he was the assistant operations officer. Once again, Petraeus's skills as an organizer and communicator who could draft concise, effective orders and supervise tactical training events were put into play. His chain of command valued his prowess, and it seemed that Petraeus's years earning a graduate education and on generals' staffs hadn't caused him to miss a step. In addition, Petraeus found being near soldiers again to be invigorating. The division was highly successful, performing very well at the CMTC, and during the REFORGER (Return of Forces to Germany) exercise. He was selected to become the brigade operations officer but only had two months in the job when he received a phone call from the Pentagon.

Petraeus's reputation as a high-performing officer was by this time well known. The call was from the army chief of staff's office, informing Petraeus that he was required to fly back to Washington to interview for the position of aide-de-camp for Chief of Staff (CSA) General Carl Vuono. Petraeus was not particularly pleased with this turn of events. Usually a rising officer like Petraeus would welcome such a high-visibility position. The CSA is typically the army's most well-known general and is responsible for all aspects of maintaining the force. While he doesn't directly lead any units in active operations, he is the face of the army within the Pentagon and usually keeps a high public profile. But Petraeus had already served General Galvin in this capacity, had spent time at West Point, and was now back on the tactical front in Germany training and preparing soldiers, which is where he wanted to be. While he could be reasonably assured of selecting a top-notch following assignment when his time as aide was concluded, he felt like he was already succeeding as a field-grade infantry officer, especially as he was the brigade S3, the most coveted major's position in the brigade. Besides, becoming Vuono's aide would mean moving Holly and the children again, away from Europe to Washington, D.C.

Much of this Petraeus couldn't say to Vuono directly, but when Petraeus did candidly indicate that the aide position wasn't one he was seeking, Vuono replied, "Good." The chief considered it an indication that Petraeus had his priorities ordered correctly. "I wouldn't want you [as aide] if you wanted the job," he told Petraeus.[1] Oftentimes aides sought the duty for self-aggrandizing reasons, and the fact that Petraeus was not enamored with the opportunity indicated he could be counted upon to keep a level head. Vuono told Petraeus to report in 30 days.

Petraeus's arrival to the chief's personal staff late in the summer of 1989, despite his reservations, reinforced the reputation he had acquired as a bit too sophisticated and eager. However, the nearly two years he would spend on the E Ring of the Pentagon with Vuono proved to be challenging but richly developmental ones. Even though Petraeus longed to return to duty in the field, he deeply respected Vuono's leadership and considered him to be a great chief, perhaps the best to lead the army in decades.

All senior generals, even the ones who consider themselves easy to work for because they listen to their staffs and take on some responsibility for their correspondence, still require a tremendous amount of direct support to massage their schedules, assist with their personal affairs, coordinate their transportation and travel, and advise and inform them on all manner of current events. It is simply the nature of the fast pace that general officers at the upper echelons of the army maintain. But in addition to these things, Vuono was not an easy man for whom to work. A career artilleryman who graduated from West Point in 1957, he was an intense man who tended to express aggravations to his closest staff officers that he could not otherwise say to others. Some days, he did not feel well and suffered from the need for a hip replacement, which he received in the summer of 1990. In August of that year, the army was ordered to begin planning to push back Iraqi dictator Saddam Hussein's invasion of Kuwait. Operations Desert Shield and Desert Storm would prove to be the largest deployment for the army in more than 20 years, and they placed enormous strain on Vuono and the army staff in the Pentagon.

Petraeus was eager to get to the Persian Gulf, and he tried all sorts of schemes to have himself sent there. Almost weekly, he asked to be released so he could be assigned to one of the deployed units in the region. Petraeus was creative. He suggested that he could best serve Vuono (and the army, and himself) by deploying. He lobbied other officers to convince the chief by pointing out that many others had been released, but it was to no avail. Vuono wouldn't take any of Petraeus's bait. Vuono simply considered Petraeus too valuable where he was. Vuono needed him, and so he would remain as the aide. As he had been for Galvin, Petraeus was a key confidant for the general. He drafted reports and testimony; assisted with speeches; and helped Vuono navigate the army's buildup in the Persian Gulf, its triumph there, and then the deployed forces' rapid de-escalation. These were heady times for the army, and leaders at all echelons enjoyed the moment, basking in the adulatory glow of a grateful public. The clouds on the horizon that suggested the army might be facing a more uncertain future were, for a short while at least, disregarded.

Stuck in the Pentagon, Petraeus could at least take solace that while working for Vuono, he had the opportunity to watch another senior leader make key decisions and to meet the army's most important and senior leaders, many of whom would later have prominent roles as policy makers in Washington. It may not have been the most enjoyable chapter of Petraeus's career, but it was nonetheless of tremendous value. He and General Vuono would remain close through the ensuing decades.

In June 1991, General Vuono announced his retirement. Petraeus would soon be able to move on, and that meant to take command of an infantry battalion, a critical assignment for a combat arms officer with high expectations.

NOTE

1. Robinson, *Tell Me How This Ends*, 59.

Chapter 7

BATTALION COMMAND
IN THE RAKKASANS

In August, 1991, Petraeus was excited to take battalion command at Fort Campbell, Kentucky, the home of the famed 101st Airborne Division. Known as the Screaming Eagles, the 101st was a storied unit and would become the one that Petraeus was most closely identified with for the rest of his career. It was activated in 1942, and its first commanding general, Major General William C. Lee, prophesied that it had a "rendezvous with destiny," which was proved to be accurate.[1] In its first major operation, the division landed behind the beaches during the June 1944 Normandy invasion, securing critical roadways and disrupting German command and control. Then six and a half months later, it fought heroically at the key town of Bastogne during the Battle of the Bulge. During the Vietnam War, its units scored some of the army's earliest tactical victories when they deployed in 1965, and again when the division deployed in late 1967. In 1968, the Screaming Eagles transitioned to helicopter-borne operations and became an airmobile division. During the army's reorganization in the 1970s, it became an air-assault formation, meaning that it was fully provided with attack and transport helicopters, and light artillery, and its troops trained to rappel into hostile landing zones. The 101st was one of the most famous divisions in the army.

The battalion of which Petraeus was assuming command was the 3d Battalion, 187th Infantry regiment. His unit, the Rakkasans, which derived its name from the Japanese word for *umbrella,* was nearly as famed as the 101st. It had fought in World War II, Korea, Vietnam, and the Persian Gulf. During the regiment's tour in occupied Japan after World War II, a translator tried to explain to local citizens how airborne soldiers operated. He chose the awkward phrase "falling down umbrella men," or *rakkasan,* and the term stuck. Earlier in the year while deployed to the Persian Gulf, the battalion had conducted what was to that point the longest air assault operation in history when in it moved by air hundreds of miles to block Iraqi forces fleeing Kuwait. The operation didn't result in a large battle, but it did demonstrate the unit's skill and toughness. Many of the troopers involved in the operation remained in the unit when Petraeus arrived.

Petraeus was overjoyed to be with combat soldiers. It was true that he had yet to deploy to an operational theater himself, but he was ready to take command and to mold the battalion in his own fashion. Like most aspiring commanders, he had been taking notes, collecting ideas, and preparing himself for this moment for many years. It was the culmination of his hard work and another important professional milestone. It was a challenging time to lead soldiers. The 1990s would prove difficult for the army.

Petraeus took command at a time when what was called a *zero defect* culture was taking hold across the army. America's victory in both the cold war and now the Persian Gulf War meant that political leaders were demanding a peace dividend. Therefore, the army was directed to reduce its forces to save money. From a high of about 780,000 at the end of the cold war, the army drew down its ranks to 480,000 by the end of the 1990s. (The army's permanent end strength as of 2010 had grown again to about 550,000.) This meant that soldiers were being dismissed at a high rate, promotions were slowed and became far more competitive than anyone had been accustomed to, and any single mistake by an officer could be career damaging. Officers were thus very cautious about how they presented themselves and their units, and they competed hard with one another to ensure that their efficiency reports were in top shape to maximize their chances for advancement and assignment to coveted positions.

Always aggressive and highly detail oriented, Petraeus worked hard to balance his competitive tendencies with an equal measure of team building. He had always been intense, and while he got along with others, he wasn't instinctively emotive with his troops. Rather, leadership was something to which he dedicated himself, and like all that he did, he was constantly striving to succeed at it. While he wasn't overly kind, he was selfless and looked out for his subordinates' well-being, attaching himself to his unit's mission so that his success and its were nearly inseparable. The result was that he both inspired loyalty and admiration in those he led and built high-performing units.

Petraeus decorated his office in Spartan fashion and hung on the wall his prized photograph of Bigeard. He enjoyed interrogating visitors about the paratrooper's identity, and of course, few at Campbell had heard of the French general. The fact that Petraeus held a PhD further separated him from the normal profile of lieutenant colonel in the division. Some of his troops whispered "doc" out of his earshot, a further note that Petraeus appeared to be from a different mold. It was evident that Petraeus would model his leadership style in ways that reflected his insatiable intellectual curiosity and drive to succeed. To his full credit, his troops always felt confident—they could easily see that Petraeus was smart, tactically expert, and influential with superior officers and that, in short, he could get things done for the battalion. And his battalion did stand out.

Soon after taking command, Petraeus distributed a standard operating procedure, or SOP, that listed in explicit detail how he expected the battalion to perform, in garrison, while training, and in the event it was deployed. One of the more innovative, or at least curious, directives was that each soldier in the battalion was to keep the top button of his battle dress uniform fastened when training in the field. In part, this was explained as a way to better camouflage exposed necks, but Petraeus's actual intent was to create a sense of identity for his men by establishing a look that was unique. It certainly wasn't very fashionable, but as Petraeus explained afterward, "It made others joke about us, which pulled us together."[2] He had decided to try out such an idea after reading about it in a novel based on his hero General Marcel Bigeard's years leading paratroopers in Vietnam and Algeria. The character in the novel and his troopers wore a distinctive lizard, or so-called Bigeard, cap that signified the wearer as belonging to an elite unit. This particular experiment wasn't one widely followed at Fort Campbell, but it showed how Petraeus thought through creative leadership techniques.

Petraeus had always been a specimen of physical fitness. At five feet nine inches and less than 155 pounds, he was a lean, wiry, and superb athlete who hadn't lost a step since his cadet days. Petraeus soon implemented a new physical fitness test, as both a yardstick to measure his soldiers and as a means to improve the performance of his battalion. It featured benchmarks much tougher to reach than the standard army test. And while Petraeus encouraged all of his soldiers to participate, the test was actually directed for the leadership. He supervised it closely, personally evaluating and grading the event when it was held several times a year. He designated the winners as Iron Rakkasans and ensured that everyone knew that he was inscribing their names on a plaque that hung at the battalion headquarters. Petraeus's name was on the top of the list, with the highest overall score.

In all that he did, Petraeus worked hard, as if each day was a series of competitions that must be won. He was a striver who had always succeeded by attacking every problem with both brawn and brains, so it was difficult to change that dynamic now. Other officers on post sometimes pointed to these characteristics of his, but Petraeus brought with him a larger reputation than many of his peers, and in many respects there was only so much he could do to mollify his critics. He was careful to keep all of his relations formally correct, and he did seek to cooperate to get missions done. Petraeus's approach simply reflected his intense preparation and ambition.

When the battalion was in the field training, Petraeus maintained high standards. He always looked impeccable. The personal equipment that every soldier donned in the field was known as an LBE, short for load-bearing equipment. The LBE consisted of a web waist belt and two canvas shoulder straps on which were hung canteens, ammo pouches, flashlights, first aid kits, and bandages. Petraeus's LBE was precisely adjusted to the standard he dictated for everyone, and it was something he closely inspected on others. He also laid out specific rules for how his command post was to operate and how reports were formatted and communicated. The result was a unit that performed well in training exercises.

Relating to his troops day to day proved to be a different kind of experience. Petraeus was a true straight arrow who had always played by the rules and had subsumed his personal interests to the culture of the army. He didn't smoke. He didn't chew tobacco. He didn't use the salty language that infantrymen typically bantered about. When a subordinate commander pointed out that Petraeus didn't wear a high-and-tight haircut that was closely shaved on the sides and slightly squared and cropped on top as was the fashion for leaders in the 101st, Petraeus welcomed the comment. He understood that one component of leadership was fitting in with others. So the next day, he arrived at headquarters with a high and tight of his own. And then he established it as the new standard for the entire battalion.

Not too long after taking command, a remarkable event occurred that would add luster to Petraeus's reputation for grit. He had directed that small-unit, live-fire maneuver training was a Rakkasan priority, and so one Saturday morning, he found his unit conducting an exercise in which squads and platoons moved up and down designated lanes, employing live ammunition and grenades to engage targets. The exercise began at 3 A.M. with a 12-mile tactical foot march before arriving at the shooting range. Although it was an orchestrated environment, the dangers were obvious and real. It was intended not only to instruct the troops about how to conduct individual movement techniques, but also to toughen them mentally by accommodating them to handling and firing live ammunition.

Petraeus and the division's assistant commander, Brigadier General Jack Keane, were observing one of the Rakkasan companies attacking a bunker complex. A soldier heaved a training grenade, armed with a small explosive charge, through a doorway and took cover while it rolled and then went off. His task complete, he began running to join his squad mates. As he moved, other soldiers provided cover by continuing to fire 5.56 mm high-velocity rounds from their M16 rifles down the range. When the grenade thrower reached his position, he flopped to the ground, using the butt of his weapon to break his fall as he had been trained. However, as his torso struck the earth, his finger was misplaced, and he accidentally pressed the trigger, launching a bullet directly at Petraeus, who grunted, stayed standing for a moment, and then went to a knee. The bullet had struck Petraeus squarely in the chest, directly above his name tag on the right side of his chest. "Dave, you are shot," Keane said as he guided Petraeus to the ground and pulled away his uniform looking for the wound.[3] From the front, it didn't look too severe. Blood was dripping through a small gash on his upper chest. But turning him over revealed a gaping wound and flowing blood. It seemed that the bullet had penetrated cleanly through Petraeus's body and there was likely severe internal damage. Clearly, Petraeus, who was awake but dazed and still unsure what had happened, was in trouble. Keane called for air medevac while the medics on-site feverishly worked to remove Petraeus's LBE. Petraeus feebly tried to protest that his carefully assembled equipment should not be cut away, but the medics ignored him as they applied pressure dressings to stop the bleeding and stabilize the wounded commander. Keane had kept Petraeus awake by speaking to him, and Petraeus had responded, "Got it," but he was now starting to go blank and appeared increasingly unaware of his surroundings.[4] Soon the medevac helo arrived to fly Petraeus to the base hospital where a doctor forcefully shoved a tube into his chest to drain fluids building up in his lung and to prevent suffocation. There was no time for anesthesia, and usually this procedure caused patients to shout out in pain—but Petraeus only grunted. A quick examination revealed that Petraeus needed specialty care unavailable at Fort Campbell. Keane phoned ahead to Vanderbilt Medical Center in Nashville, one of the nation's premier medical facilities. Dr. Bill Frist, chief of thoracic surgery and soon to be elected a U.S. senator from Tennessee, was the surgeon summoned to attend Petraeus. His exam revealed that the round had taken away part of the right lung and damaged an artery. The ensuing surgery took a full six hours, but Frist successfully stabilized Petraeus. It had been a close call.

The medical team advised Petraeus that recovery would take about 10 weeks and that he would need to move ahead cautiously. Naturally, Petraeus had a more ambitious timeline in mind, and with his battalion already preparing for a large field exercise within the month, he wanted to return to duty as soon as he could. While Holly admonished him to be prudent, Petraeus, who was released back to the hospital at

Fort Campbell, harangued the staff to accelerate his release from medical care. He even got down to do push-ups in his room to impress them with his strength. Finally, a doctor permitted him to heal at home, but Petraeus quickly exceeded the restrictions he had been given. When he went to the gym to try running, it caused his lung to bleed and prompted a stern warning from his doctor. There could be very real and lasting consequences if he pushed too hard, too fast. Petraeus was barely deterred, however, and just a month later, he was back at the head of his battalion for an emergency deployment exercise that included an air assault operation to seize an airfield at Fort Bragg, North Carolina. And he soon confirmed that he could run almost as fast and as long as ever, which of course included his direct leadership in postwide athletic competitions that resulted in championships in football, softball, and cross-country. It had been a remarkable journey to the brink and back.

This example of Petraeus's resiliency, instead of being framed in the context of an unfortunate training accident, was over the succeeding years burnished into a narrative of genuine fortitude in the face of personal adversity. The incident was sometimes talked about by his admirers as if it were even a welcome test of strength. It was offered as a tale providing evidence that Petraeus was surely destined for grand achievements in the future, and it became closely tied to his personal and professional identity. Ultimately, however, it was a case in which the truth needed no molding; the reality itself was truly astonishing.

NOTES

1. U.S. Army, "101st Airborne Division (Air Assault)," *Fort Campbell, Kentucky,* http://www.campbell.army.mil/UNITS/101ST/Pages/default.aspx.

2. Cloud and Jaffe, *The Fourth Star*, 94.

3. General Jack Keane, interview with the author, June 10, 2010.

4. Ibid.

Chapter 8

OPERATIONS IN HAITI

The remainder of Petraeus's battalion command passed successfully as he and his unit added to its reputation for pressing limits and training hard. Petraeus changed command in July 1993, when General Keane brought him up to serve on the division staff as the G3, or operations officer. Keane was driving the division hard, and he knew he could rely on Petraeus. As the G3, Petraeus brought the full weight of his energy as a planner and trainer to bear, directing no less than five deployments by division units to the army's combat training centers, establishing new standards of excellence for a division headquarters during a major battle command exercise, deploying soldiers to Somalia to conduct humanitarian and combat operations, and conducting disaster relief operations in local communities in western Kentucky and northern Tennessee to help them recover from severe ice storms. He and Keane formed a close relationship that would play an important role years later in the debate about U.S. troop levels in Iraq. It would be Keane who became an early and vocal advocate for the reinforcement of U.S. forces there, and it would be Petraeus who would lead them in 2007 as the overall American commander in the country.

In the meantime, as his time with the 101st wound down, Petraeus began to plan for his next assignment. Officers who finished command and were in the top echelon of their cohorts were typically slated to attend one of the armed forces senior service colleges. The purpose of these schools is to educate promising officers in the art of strategy and high-level policy formulation, and to expose them to members of other services and to the broader workings of the U.S. government. The army, navy, and air force each possessed a university, and two in Washington, D.C., were sponsored by the National Defense University. But with a PhD already in hand, Petraeus didn't want to attend one of the formal institutions with a standard curriculum. Rather, he sought a more individual course of instruction and chose to attend a fellowship at Georgetown University for the upcoming academic year.

The topic Petraeus chose for his research was U.S. policy toward Haiti, a subject of great interest at the time because that country was teetering on the brink of chaos. After a 1991 coup, the country's president, Jean-Bertrand Aristide, had gone into exile. After a series of negotiations between Haiti's military leaders and the Clinton administration, a plan was being developed to restore a democratic government with the assistance of U.S. forces. But there was much hesitation in Washington, both in the Pentagon and in the White House, about the prospect of sending troops to a dysfunctional, third-world country. The memory of the October 1993 battle in Mogadishu, Somalia, in which U.S. soldiers were forced into a bloody two-day firefight burned brightly in everyone's memory. That event had prompted President Clinton to abruptly withdraw American forces, and nobody wanted another misadventure. The Pentagon was arguing that any deployment must feature overwhelming force and that the political objectives must be limited. U.S. troops would get in, establish security, and then turn the entire operation over to the United Nations.

Petraeus obtained an interview with Deputy Secretary of State Strobe Talbott who was closely working on the Haiti problem. After talking to Petraeus, Talbott invited him to attend a full-day meeting on U.S. strategy for Haiti in the White House Conference Center. Petraeus took it all in, noting how senior diplomats and security council advisors asked questions and defined their positions. It was his first direct exposure to the nexus between military, diplomatic, and political policy-making communities that he would know intimately just about a decade later.

A few months prior to that session, Operation Uphold Democracy had begun in September 1994 with the unopposed landing of a U.S.-led multinational force numbering more than 20,000 Americans and some 2,000 contingent members from more than a dozen countries. They immediately set out to restore civil administration, provide for limited essential services, and begin training local security forces.

Petraeus sensed an opportunity to become more directly involved in an ongoing contingency operation. Learning of his interest and work on Haiti, Major General Joe Kinzer (U.S. Army), who was designated to command the UN forces, called Petraeus and asked Petraeus to join him on the mission. Petraeus responded that he'd be honored to do it if Kinzer could gain the necessary army approvals for him to leave his fellowship. Having missed deployment to the Gulf War, he viewed the upcoming Haiti operation as a long-sought opportunity to be on the front lines with U.S. troops. It might not be a hot war zone, but it was the nearest thing available.

Permission to deploy soon arrived, and he flew to Haiti in early 1995, in advance of the U.S. hand over of the mission to the UN that was scheduled for the end of March. At that point, a sizeable U.S. contingent would remain in Haiti to continue to advance America's limited objectives. In addition to U.S. Special Forces teams, regular army troops from the 10th Mountain Division and then the 25th Infantry Division, formed the core of the American effort. When Petraeus hit the ground, there was an enormous amount to be done and only a bare-bones staff at the multinational headquarters.

Petraeus dived into work, directing all of his planning talents and high energy at scaling the mountain of requirements. He oversaw the crafting of detailed plans covering roles and missions for the UN force, civil relations, and logistics. One of the most important steps was the identification of rules of engagement that outlined the parameters by which U.S. and UN troops would act on the island. He produced a lengthy manual of SOPs, reminiscent of the kind of document he produced as a battalion commander, outlining the many dos and don'ts for the force. And as more and more officers arrived, he initiated a training course to orient the new arrivals on the situation on the ground and create a common understanding about Haiti.

In every way, Petraeus demonstrated his creativity. His academic background helped him to dialogue with civilian aid groups and UN officials, and he learned how to communicate effectively with senior military and political leaders in Washington who peppered the headquarters with demands for reports and information. He supervised training programs for the police, sought funding to build schools and civic buildings, and helped to coordinate transportation and support for raids targeting criminal elements that still disrupted stability in the major towns. Petraeus even found a novel way to restore power to key parts of Port-au-Prince: he sent a staff officer to the foreign embassies in the capital, seeking donations to purchase generators. It worked, at least as a stopgap solution. Most important of all, he sought with Major General Kinzer's approval to push the concept of assigning UN forces to actually live among the local population, a concept that only U.S. Special Forces had practiced until the UN took over. Security and reconstruction could only be assured when the UN forces were visible in the city's neighborhoods, so he labored to make its implementation possible.

From week to week, the American and UN presence made security gains. The killing squads that had been assassinating government employees still operated but were at least curtailed, and a bare modicum of economic activity had returned. Nonetheless, violence continued, and widespread destitution was the norm. There was little electricity, the courts barely functioned, and poverty was rampant. As Petraeus later reflected, "There were just a handful of us, literally less the fingers on one hand, pulling this thing together."[1]

When Petraeus redeployed in June, he was convinced that he had established the framework in Haiti for the kind of contingency deployments that would characterize the future security environment. His time there deepened his understanding of peacekeeping operations and pointed out in the starkest terms the enormous tasks involved with nation building. The army would need to master this kind of operation and could not afford to assemble its components ad hoc as he had been compelled to do. He and Colonel Bob Killebrew, who had participated in the Haiti deployment with Petraeus, coauthored an optimistic journal article that stated in part that, "in detail of planning and degree of coordination the effort to stand Haiti back up after taking it down broke new ground. . . . An environment conducive to political, social and economic development has been created in Haiti."[2] He was typically optimistic about what had been sustainably accomplished, but for Petraeus, it had indeed been a successful contingency effort that served as a laboratory for many of his ideas about how the army must be ready to operate in the post–cold war world.

NOTES

1. Cloud and Jaffe, *The Fourth Star*, 99.
2. Ibid.

Chapter 9

BRIGADE COMMAND AT FORT BRAGG

Petraeus would have liked to remain in Haiti, but he was due for his next major assignment, as commander of the 1st Brigade of the 82d Airborne Division at Fort Bragg, North Carolina, nicknamed the Devil Brigade. His brigade consisted primarily of units from the 504th Parachute Infantry Regiment, the first airborne regiment in the 82d. Like the 101st, with whom Petraeus closely identified, the 82d boasted a rich history as an elite formation. Known as the All Americans because members of the division came from all 48 states in the Union at the time of its founding, it fought in three major campaigns in World War I. It was inactivated during the interwar years and reconstituted in 1942 for World War II. It then became the army's premier airborne unit, conducting parachute and glider assaults into Sicily and Salerno, Italy, before transferring to northern Europe, where it fought in Normandy, Holland, Belgium, and Germany. Over the succeeding decades, the division deployed a number of times, including to Central America, Vietnam, Grenada, Panama, and the Persian Gulf. The division's paratroopers had a reputation for being some of the toughest soldiers in the army, and command of one of its major subordinate units was a plum assignment. Petraeus knew he would find fresh challenges at Fort Bragg.

Although he wasn't officially due to be promoted for several more months, at a ceremony in Haiti before he departed, he had already been frocked to the rank of full colonel. This allowed him to arrive at Fort Bragg already wearing his new silver eagles, a gesture afforded officers entering key positions to reinforce their authority. The 1st Brigade was currently commanded by Colonel John Abizaid, another rising star in the army and a highly respected leader who would play a role in Petraeus's career again later when Abizaid would be America's overall commander in the Middle East.

Like Petraeus, Abizaid had charted a unique career as an infantryman, one that included both significant academic accomplishments and real-world military experience. He is the grandson of Lebanese immigrants and is a native Arabic speaker who long advocated that U.S. forces be trained and ready for both offensive operations as well as peacekeeping missions. Abizaid earned a master's degree in Middle Eastern studies at Harvard and was an Olmsted Scholar at the University of Jordan in Amman, Jordan. Abizaid also had operational experience, commanding a ranger company during the 1983 invasion of Grenada and deploying his battalion to northern Iraq to protect the Kurds from Iraqi deprivations in 1991.

Petraeus's leadership style, however, was much different from Abizaid's and, for that matter, was typically more intense than most other commanders. Once he was in command, as he had done each time he was in a position of authority, Petraeus set about establishing new procedures and devoted his attention to all manner of details, often conducting troop inspections himself. Petraeus trusted his noncommissioned officers (NCOs) to directly supervise individual soldier matters, but he also saw it as his duty to check himself. He did empower his NCOs in novel ways, to include mortar and artillery methods that were more responsive to calls for fire. And he pressed his staff to institute more creative training scenarios. He oversaw the construction of a mock village so that live-fire training in an urban environment could be exercised. Other training events focused on peacekeeping and nation-building problems that the brigade would likely face in a deployment like Haiti. He also returned to a vigorous physical training regimen that some leaders found hard to keep up with. It was a testament to Petraeus's rigor, since the culture at Fort Bragg fostered extraordinary pride in being the best and never saying quit. As had been the case at Fort Campbell, there were some who thought that Petraeus was simply driving too hard, but he stuck to his standards. Petraeus adhered to them personally as well, so the complaints, while persistent, didn't carry much weight. Petraeus pressed ahead, molding his brigade as he saw fit. He tried to impart a sense of mental agility and to ensure that his troops possessed wide-ranging expertise because it wasn't clear what kinds of missions they might be called upon to face. The general atmosphere in the army was still one of uncertainty, making the jobs of commanders like Petraeus very difficult. While it was evident that changes to the army were forthcoming, the debate about their direction continued unabated.

Petraeus's general view, like that held by many in the army, was that the U.S. military's dominance of ground warfare, in terms of its superior weapons platforms and tremendous maneuver skills, made it unlikely that a future opponent would seek to challenge America in a classic, force-on-force fight. The images of Saddam Hussein's army, its vaunted Soviet-designed tanks burning by the thousands in the Kuwaiti desert, and its infantry fleeing pell-mell were fresh in the minds of military thinkers worldwide. Only a fool or a leader bent on military suicide would venture a similar challenge.

A new vision of future war was thus needed. Billions of dollars were tied to this debate because the concept about the future that prevailed would lead to massive investments in equipment and infrastructure. The Pentagon's official response, termed *Joint Vision 2010*, was unveiled in 1996. It was the first sweeping statement since the end of the cold war about the security challenges facing the United States and how America's armed forces would organize to confront them. JV 2010 was remarkably ambitious. It was heavily dependent on technological solutions to war, taking the unfounded and ahistorical position that the tempo of combat would now be determined by a technology-driven cycle: Superior information possessed by U.S. forces about the battlefield would mean that U.S. forces could make quicker and better decisions. Superior decision making would in turn allow U.S. forces to move with great speed and agility to establish superior positional advantage by outmaneuvering any foe. Finally, with better information, decisions, and position, U.S. forces would achieve new levels of lethality through precise targeting of enemy vulnerabilities. The result would be unmatched, and unmatchable, U.S. dominance. JV 2010 went on to infer that because U.S. forces would pack so much punch, their size, especially the land-power elements, could be reduced. Precision strikes could substitute for boots on the ground. It was a doctrine conveniently suited to Americans' infatuation with technical solutions to every problem.

The problem with JV 2010, as Petraeus and more thoughtful historians and strategists well knew, was that the landscape of the 1990s didn't seem to feature conflicts subject to precision-dominant weapons. And it was not likely that any succeeding decade would accommodate the vision either. Instead, military leaders were confronted with collapsing nation-states, ethnic unrest, and humanitarian crises. There seemed to be an abundance of challenges—like the deterioration of Haiti, or the unrest in Somalia, or the political repression against the Kurds—more than there were enemies that looked like those in JV 2010.

While the Pentagon moved in the direction of JV 2010, within units across the army it was increasingly evident that soldiers needed training in new skills. Whether the mission was to provide food and medical care in politically contested regions, disrupt international criminal organizations, reconstitute civil infrastructure, or topple a dictator or prevent genocide, troops like Petraeus's would have to accomplish many different kinds of tasks. Hence Petraeus devoted himself to training excellence with an eye toward such diversity. On a rotation at the Joint Readiness Training Center in Arkansas, his troops actually defeated the vaunted Opposing Forces, or OpFor (highly skilled U.S. units that played the role of an enemy force) in the center's new urban warfare facility. Petraeus's soldiers also earned a victory during a defensive mission, a very rare achievement for a U.S. brigade given the difficulty of the training scenario.

As Petraeus trained his troops, at Fort Bragg as elsewhere, he continued to exhibit a trait that separated him from most of his peers. The classic orientation of an army leader was to focus downward, devoting all energies to the betterment of his unit. Officers had long understood that a singular focus on the fundamentals of soldiering: training, inspecting, team building, and leader development, were the foundation of all high-performing units. It was how the army had righted itself after the morass of the Vietnam experience. Petraeus did this too, in spades. But unlike most of his peers, Petraeus also kept his head up, always sensing the messages being given by senior army and defense officials. He looked further ahead than most because he recognized sooner than others of his station that the further up in rank he rose, the more important would be his ability to navigate the positions staked out by those in Washington. To aid him, Petraeus continued to nurture and grow networks of like-minded people who might be able to enable his ambitions. In addition to his relationships with fellow officers with whom he had served in the 101st and in Haiti, he stayed active in the influential Sosh Department and Princeton alumni networks, as well as with his connections from the Pentagon, Georgetown, and increasingly, with those in other government agencies in the capital region. It was a formidable and helpful asset that would ultimately pay dividends when he needed support from across the government to implement his plans to surmount the difficult challenges of Iraq.

Chapter 10

AN INJURY AND DEPLOYMENT TO THE BALKANS

When Petraeus completed brigade command in the summer of 1997, he once again became a senior staff officer in the Pentagon. Initially, he was the executive assistant to the director of the Joint Staff and then in October began a nearly two-year assignment as executive assistant to the chairman of the Joint Chiefs, General Hugh Shelton. The primary responsibility of the chairman is to provide military advice to the president. The Joint Staff supports the chairman in this endeavor and serves as the liaison between the service staffs and the combatant commanders who lead the armed services on operations around the world. Petraeus's position as Shelton's assistant placed him once again near the center of every important defense-related issue that passed through the Pentagon. As the chairman's exec, Petraeus assisted with key U.S. military operations underway around the world, including the Kosovo air campaign, the pursuit of Bosnian war criminals, Operations Desert Fox and Desert Thunder in the Gulf, and the United States' deliberations concerning the pursuit of a figure who would eventually become infamous, Osama bin Laden, in Sudan and Afghanistan. Petraeus's success in these endeavors virtually guaranteed promotion to brigadier general, a major step up in rank, which indeed arrived in January 2000.

There are several thousand colonels in the army, but only several hundred generals.

Petraeus had departed the Pentagon in the summer of 1999, destined for Fort Bragg once again, where this time he was to be the assistant division commander for operations. In that capacity, he would be second in command to the division commander and would be in charge of supervising the training and employment of the division's troops to any contingency. It was another sign that Petraeus was right on track professionally.

It was at Fort Bragg in 2000 that Petraeus suffered a second serious accident. Like the shooting incident on the firing range at Fort Campbell years before, this one also came close to not only sidelining his career, but also inflicting potentially life-changing injuries. Always seeking adventure and further challenges, and an avid parachutist, Petraeus drove to nearby Raeford to practice jumps with the army's Golden Knights skydiving team. The Golden Knights are the army's premier demonstration skydiving team and serve as goodwill ambassadors around the world. They have a reputation as the best in the world, and so Petraeus enjoyed jumping with them.

One afternoon on the last jump of the day, his chute lost its lift during a low-altitude turn and collapsed, causing him to plummet to the ground. The doctors in the intensive care unit of Fort Bragg's Womack Army Medical Center delivered the news—Petraeus's pelvis was severely fractured both in the front and rear. Initially, he and Holly had a choice to make: Recovery could occur while Petraeus was kept lying still and flat on his back for many weeks to allow the bones to heal and fuse together gradually. Or surgery could be performed to bolt the major bones together, reducing recovery time. In the end, X-rays showed that surgery was imperative due to the displacement of the bones and the necessity to pull them back into alignment. Even with the surgery, it would be a lengthy trip back to normal movement. It was too soon to tell if Petraeus would recover full motion and whether he could again take up physical training and sports, especially running.

With orders to remain on crutches for three months and not to climb any more than a single flight of stairs each day, he was discharged. Holly set up a hospital bed on the first floor of their home, complete with a trapeze bar over it so that he could maneuver without risking reinjury.

He had recently been given the position of chief of staff for the XVIII Airborne Corps, an important duty responsible for directly supporting the commanding general of the corps by supervising the entire corps staff and garrison at Fort Bragg. Petraeus was agitated that he had been sidelined and was eager to return to his duties. Any form of inactivity frustrated him. Besides, he was doing well professionally and felt driven to stay on the job. There were only a handful of division commands that would become open in the next few years, and he very much wanted to command a division. It was division command that separated generals who would retire in their current grade from those who would advance to three- and four-star rank.

Initially, other officers on the staff assisted with Petraeus's workload. He started by working half days, gradually extending his hours in the office and increasingly violating his doctors' orders to rest. While still on crutches, he led the corps through a major command post exercise, garnering favorable feedback from the army's senior leadership. Within weeks, he was fully back on his feet. Remarkably, only a year and a half later, he would run the army's annual 10-mile race in Washington, completing the course in less than 64 minutes. In typical Petraeus fashion, another astonishing recovery was unfolding that added even further polish to what was becoming an aura of his invincibility. Petraeus's fierce competitive streak, his innate sense of timing and powerful intellect, combined with the networks of professional allies he cultivated, continued to propel him forward. While some accused him of being career-minded, Petraeus's demeanor was more complex than that. His passion for achievement did burn bright, but he was always an avid student of the profession who sincerely wanted to be the best possible leader, and he strictly adhered to the core values of the officer corps. He believed, and did his utmost to live, West Point's motto of Duty, Honor, and Country. He was creative and tenacious, and he demanded excellence, in himself and in others. If he found it difficult to suppress his drive to compete, and if his natural talents were superior to most, such were the dynamic tensions with which he wrestled.

In 2001, Petraeus deployed to the Balkans as a part of the NATO-led Operation Joint Forge. His titles were assistant chief of staff for operations for NATO's Stabilization Force (SFOR), and then deputy commander, U.S. Joint Interagency Counter Terrorism Task Force. SFOR was the multinational peacekeeping force in Bosnia-Herzegovina that was tasked with upholding the Dayton Agreement fashioned in 1995 ending the war in the territories of the former Yugoslavia. By the time Petraeus arrived, the Balkans may have been receding from the headlines of U.S. newspapers, but it remained a priority theater for the army. The hunt for war criminals, which Petraeus directly oversaw as the deputy commanding general, was the army's largest special operations and intelligence deployment in the world at the time. Army Chief of Staff Erik Shinseki personally selected Petraeus for this important responsibility, one that would prove illuminating to Petraeus in the years ahead when he would be asked to harness the talents and resources of these critical U.S. defense assets in the Middle East. Now cooperating with British and French partners in the Balkans, the operations Petraeus oversaw witnessed more war criminals detained than ever before. Petraeus traveled to Allied capitals throughout Europe to coordinate these operations, including to Belgrade to meet with Serbian prime minister Zoran Djindjic.

After the terrorist attacks of September 11, 2001, the U.S. Defense Department shifted its attention to waging the first stages of the Global War on Terror (GWOT). In the Balkans, this took the form of understanding and interdicting Islamic radicals who were operating on the side of the Muslim Bosnians against the Orthodox Serbs and identifying and disrupting terrorists' complex relationships and networks extending across the region. Petraeus oversaw the expansion of military authorities to seek out war criminals and terrorists and so continued the hard work of mapping their cells and networks in southern Europe. This led to significant gains in the early years of America's war on terrorism.

By the time his year's deployment was over, Petraeus was ready to get back to the United States. He wanted to be in the middle of what was clearly going to be an escalation of the GWOT. When he learned that he was to be promoted to major general and become the commanding general of the 101st Airborne Division at Fort Campbell, he was thrilled. His hard work and determination—and a bit of luck—had led him to another success.

Chapter 11

COMMANDING GENERAL OF THE SCREAMING EAGLES: LEADING THE 101ST AIRBORNE DIVISION (AIR ASSAULT) IN IRAQ

While America's defense community was deliberating about the threats facing the nation, the future arrived much sooner and in a way that nobody expected. Most Americans spent the 1990s concentrating on domestic affairs. The deployment of U.S. forces to Somalia and Haiti captured the public's attention for a period but then receded as global economic expansion seemed to be sweeping former antagonisms aside. But unnoticed by westerners, enormous tensions were building. In the Middle East, the United States had become the predominant geopolitical power. It maintained a substantial military footprint in Kuwait, which still depended on American forces to defend against the unpredictable Saddam Hussein in Iraq. American warplanes continued to patrol the skies of Iraq in accordance with UN resolutions. In the rest of the region, America's presence was also highly visible. Close relationships grew between the United States and the rulers of the Gulf states as well as with the royal family of Saudi Arabia. America was viewed by the governing class of the Middle East as perhaps an unwanted, but still necessary partner. America brought a measure of stability not only by serving as a bulwark against Iraq, but also by acting as a bulwark from the agitations routinely perpetrated by Iran. Besides, it just seemed to make sense to sustain cordial relations with the world's sole superpower.

However, America's presence had other, unintended, consequences. A generation of young men felt trapped by the corrupt dictatorships that governed them and stifled economic and cultural opportunities. This was nothing new to the region—the Islamic world had been dominated by stagnant regimes for many years. Momentously, in the 1990s those not satisfied with the status quo for the first time had wide-ranging access to media outlets, especially the Internet. What they saw there was a vast disparity between the lives they were forced to lead and the seemingly unlimited prosperity offered elsewhere. Their solution was not to imitate the political and social values that they saw, but rather to target the Western nations, and especially the United States. Through a prism of religious extremism, they accused the United States of supporting the regimes that were oppressing Muslims. Hence, the best way to topple their near enemy—hated regimes in Riyadh, Cairo, and Amman, to say nothing of Jerusalem—was to attack the far enemy that supported these governments—the United States. Unable to compete against conventional forces, they formed extensive terrorist cells that eventually became an international network. Chief among them was the group Al Qaeda, which made the shrewd decision to wage asymmetric war against the United States.

Petraeus assumed command of the 101st Division in the summer of 2002. The autumn and winter were a whirlwind of activity at Fort Campbell, as Petraeus pushed his subordinates to prepare for what became increasingly imminent—an invasion of Iraq. Elements of the division had recently fought in Afghanistan, so it already possessed a nucleus of combat veterans. Despite this, the magnitude of the necessary preparations was extensive. Leaders focused their attention on the imperatives of command and control, exercising their ability to write and communicate orders, while the noncommissioned officers led their troops to maintain and pack vehicles and equipment, while training on their assigned weapons. The overall focus for the division was to be sure that they could operate in a desert environment. The likelihood that they might have to fight in Iraq's cities was well understood, but training for urban combat was difficult, and there was always room for improvement.

While the 101st trained, war preparations at the national level moved forward. In early February 2003, Secretary of State Colin Powell briefed the UN Security Council regarding the threat allegedly posed by Iraq in terms of its programs to develop weapons of mass destruction (WMD). Powell employed several pieces of intelligence that later proved to be more coincidental than conclusive, but at the time, the majority of the members of the intelligence community in Washington did believe that Saddam Hussein possessed some level of WMD capability. Hussein's persistent defiance of UN resolutions in recent years added fuel to the argument that he was a dangerous leader who could no longer be tolerated in the post–9/11 security environment.

Through the winter, preparations to launch an attack into Iraq proceeded. Even while politicians and diplomats debated their positions and crafted policy, the Pentagon continued to deploy forces into the Middle East. A brigade from the 82d Airborne Division and most of Petraeus's 101st Airborne Division (Air Assault) arrived in Kuwait, joining the 3d Infantry Division, which had been in theater already for some time. These units would make up the bulk of the combat power of the U.S. Army's V Corps. In early March, the U.S. Marine's 1st Division as well as the 1st Armoured Division of the United Kingdom had also arrived. The Pentagon's plan also called for the U.S. 4th Infantry Division to invade Iraq from the north, but this required Turkey's acquiescence. U.S. leaders assumed that Turkey, as a member of NATO, would agree, but ultimately, permission was denied, meaning that the 4th Infantry Division had to change plans and travel to Kuwait. It would arrive too late to participate in the initial assault. At Secretary of Defense Donald Rumsfeld's insistence, the invasion plans were reworked. Now there would only be a southern avenue of approach for the attacking Coalition units.

On 17 March, President Bush gave Saddam Hussein an ultimatum, which Hussein ignored. Two days later, a missile strike launched at Hussein missed but signaled the start of the war. After a short but intense air campaign, Coalition forces launched the ground invasion on 20 March when they crossed the berm separating Kuwait from Iraq. Their chief objective was to destroy Hussein's Baathist Party regime, which had ruled Iraq for decades. The regime adhered to the Sunni branch of Islam and hence persecuted all other minorities, including Shia Muslims, Christians, and ethnic minorities like the Kurds, Assyrians, and Turkomans.

The invasion plan was ambitious. It was essentially a very long raid that would expose the flanks of U.S. and Coalition troops along a nearly

300-mile line of communication between Kuwait and the invasion's objective, Baghdad. Other subordinate but important objectives were the
discovery of whatever WMD stocks existed and the preservation of Iraq's
oil infrastructure. The Pentagon did not want a repeat of the Gulf War,
when retreating Iraqi troops set afire vast tracks of Kuwait's oil fields,
costing billions of dollars and inflicting substantial ecological damage
to the region.

The invasion started well. The 3d Infantry Division promptly captured Tallil air base on the outskirts of An Nasiriyah after a 90-mile attack. But as it consolidated its position, the division began encountering
Iraqi paramilitary forces in significant numbers. Some of these were simply criminal elements, but most were members of the *fedayeen* ("one who
sacrifices himself"), a paramilitary organization loyal to Hussein and
the Baathists. They were poorly trained but were fanatical and, as they
wore civilian clothing, could blend into the local population. Although
they possessed only light weapons, such as AK-47 assault rifles, rocket-
propelled grenades, and sometimes, mortars, they proved dangerous to un-
suspecting Coalition troops. Resistance popped up in many of Iraq's cities,
prompting V Corps' commanding general Lieutenant General William
Wallace to comment, "The enemy we're fighting is different from the
one we war gamed against."[1] It was a true statement, but not one that
found favor in the Pentagon where the story was that the invasion was
proceeding strictly according to plan. While the fedayeen's resistance
startled the Coalition troops in the first week of the invasion and they inflicted some casualties, the Shiites of southern Iraq showed limited toler-
ance for them as it became clear that Hussein's regime was faltering and
would likely topple. Nonetheless, a model for resistance to the invaders
had been established that would cause tremendous difficulties for the Coalition later.

Petraeus was confident in himself and his soldiers, and when the 101st
received its orders, he and the division were ready, having marshaled in
Kuwait's western desert before crossing the border. This was a personally
intense moment for him. For the first time in his 30 years in uniform, he
would be leading troops in combat. The 101st, while an air assault division, was to move much of its assets on the ground. Its convoys consisted of more than 500 vehicles organized into march units, each with a
distinct mission and between 50 and 200 vehicles in length. There were

few armored, tracked vehicles such as M1 Abrams tanks and Bradley fighting vehicles—the 101st had to assign these from attached units, so its troops would mostly go forward in wheeled and soft-skinned vehicles. To win, it would depend primarily on speed, agility, and the lethality of its attack helicopters.

For several days, 17,000 Screaming Eagle troops traveled north, pressing deep into the relentless desert, stopping only to sip fuel from the accompanying tanker trucks and to rotate exhausted drivers. The division had been assigned a critical, if supporting, role to play in the overall American plan for the first phase of combat operations. As the division had done during the Gulf War, it was given the mission to secure the flanks of the corps, conduct reconnaissance to identify Iraqi strongpoints, and then establish forward operating bases southwest of Baghdad to enable the final attack against the capital. Driving forward, Petraeus's men bypassed many small villages, launching several deep attacks with their Apache attack helicopter battalions whenever concentrations of the Iraqi army could be located. Organized Iraqi resistance crumbled as Coalition troops pressed ahead.

Paramilitary fighters, however, persisted to strike at the extended U.S. formations. Petraeus was given the mission to take the 101st to clear them out from An Najaf, Karbala, and Al Hillah, each sizeable cities. While the leading Coalition forces largely bypassed these places, they harbored large numbers of enemy fighters whom Petraeus and the 101st were ordered to neutralize. Al Hillah, the smallest, was a town of more than 300,000 residents. Karbala and An Najaf were two to three times as large. Clearly, the elements of the 101st along with elements of the 82d operating in the area would not be enough to systematically attack these cities. Rather, Coalition forces would have to conduct fast, hard strikes against any resistance. Petraeus proved himself to be a capable combat commander. In each place, Petraeus's troops, which included the Rakkasans he had commanded years earlier, routed any remaining Iraqi army units and subdued pockets of fedayeen after several sharp engagements.

At Najaf, a city of more than a half million about 150 miles south of Baghdad, Petraeus ran into a sharp battle with enemy fighters. Adding to the confusion of the battlefield, a strong sandstorm had erupted, further limiting visibility and hampering the situational understanding of the 101st's leaders, from Petraeus all the way down to the division's squad leaders. Iraqi fighters typically hid in positions along the sides of roads, taking cover in ditches and behind trees and objects along the shoulders. They permitted any armored vehicles at the lead of the 101st's columns to move past, waiting for the soft-skinned trucks filled with infantry to appear. Then several fedayeen would spring an ambush consisting of rocket propelled grenades or machine guns, and sometimes hand grenades. Even though Petraeus's soldiers traveled through cities with weapons at the ready, countering these attacks was difficult. It was simply impossible to march on foot through extensive built-up areas to root out each individual guerrilla.

Petraeus's mission was to stop these fedayeen, who had been conducting lethal, often suicide, attacks either on foot or mounted in the back of pickup trucks, against U.S. truck columns that were driving along a key road that passed by the city. Intelligence reports suggested that there were more than 1,000 enemy fighters in the area, a number that didn't threaten the 101st's combat formations directly but was a formidable obstacle to the line of communication and supply for U.S. forces that were already operating farther north. Initially, it wasn't clear who the enemy was: "Who is it that's fighting?" Petraeus remembered asking later.[2] He knew they were likely fedayeen, but there could also be foreign fighters, Iraqi army troops, or a combination of all three. He could not know for certain, and whatever their composition, Petraeus knew that he needed to eliminate the threat quickly so he could keep his own division moving ahead. But he cherished the lives of his troops and did not want to throw them into hasty fights through the warrens and back alleys of Najaf. At the same time, he couldn't afford massive artillery barrages that would flatten large tracts of the city and alienate the population.

Petraeus recognized that the fedayeen and their allies did not represent the majority in any neighborhood, and artillery would inadvertently cause a large number of civilian casualties. This would create even greater resistance as the Iraqis would resent the suffering caused by such heavy-handed tactics. The few fedayeen that would be killed in the process of an artillery strike weren't worth the long-term consequences. He insisted that the division maneuver aggressively to cut off fedayeen wherever they could be found and eliminate using direct fires. Thus he ordered one brigade to take up strong defensive positions along the highway. Over the next few days, the 101st fired rockets, mortar, and artillery on enemy fighters who could be identified, but only if the targets were clear. Meanwhile, coordinated infantry assaults flushed out the enemy. More and more of the fedayeen were being killed, and their desire to do battle with the Americans was waning. Finally, some of the 101st's accompanying M1 tanks dashed into the city, drawing out the enemy and providing the opportunity to respond with overwhelming fire, breaking the resistance.

As Petraeus told one of his commanders later that day, "The good news is that we now own Najaf. . . . And the bad news is that we now own Najaf."[3] Although he requested food, water, and basic provisions be transported to the city for the local population, Coalition logistics trains were barely keeping up with the advancing military formations. The 101st had to move on, and the civilians of Najaf would have to wait for succor. As much as they could, Petraeus's soldiers provided water and fuel for generators and consolidated out of harm's way the large amounts of small arms, ammunition, and military supplies they inevitably captured from Iraqi military compounds. Then they pushed on.

Aided by Apache helicopter raids conducted by the 101st, the 3d Infantry Division pushed through the Karbala Gap on 1 April, a natural choke point guarding the crossing sites at the Euphrates River and the approaches to Baghdad. Three days later, U.S. troops captured the international airport on the western edge of the city. After American forces conducted the famous *thunder runs*, during which armored columns penetrated deep within the city on high-speed dashes with guns blazing, organized resistance by Iraqis, both the army and any remaining paramilitary fighters fighting on behalf of Saddam's regime, burned itself out. By 9 April, the Iraqi government had fallen, and the Americans found themselves in charge of Iraq, at least militarily.

As far as many military commanders and their political bosses were concerned, the occupation of Baghdad signaled a successful conclusion to the operation. In the first flush of military triumph, there was widespread belief that a rapid withdrawal would commence as the Iraqi population welcomed—and thanked—their new occupiers. Petraeus and more reflective leaders knew otherwise. A careful student of war, such as Petraeus, could tell right away that America faced an enormous reconstruction task. He understood full well that a victorious invader quickly turns, in the eyes of the local population, into a resented occupier. There was no shortcut to the extensive requirements that would be asked of the U.S. ground forces in Iraq. Civilian teams of humanitarian workers and a dedicated cadre of diplomats would not be enough. For both the sake of the Iraqis' well-being, for which the Coalition bore responsibility, as well as to prevent any loosely governed space in which terrorists could operate, the next steps that were taken to stabilize Iraq would be critical.

But for the moment at least, the feeling on the U.S. side was one of contentment at the brave and skilled performance of its armed forces. Petraeus and his division had performed well. They had played an important, if not decisive, role during the invasion. Once again, America had clearly demonstrated that it could attack and dominate a formidable opponent. Saddam Hussein's vaunted army had been dispatched with relative ease. However, America's sense of satisfaction would prove to be short lived.

NOTES

1. Jim Dwyer, "A Gulf Commander Sees a Longer Road," *New York Times*, March 28, 2003, http://www.nytimes.com/2003/03/28/interna tional/worldspecial/28GENE.html.

2. Cloud and Jaffe, *The Fourth Star*, 116.

3. Ibid.

Chapter 12

NORTH TO MOSUL
WITH THE 101ST

The fall of Baghdad to the American-led Coalition forces in early April signaled the beginning of a new phase of the conflict. But far from being the decisive operation, the invasion that culminated in the defeat of Saddam Hussein's government would eventually be seen as merely the opening act of a long and painful endeavor. While the final throngs of resistance fighters were being defeated in Baghdad, American forces began to receive reports that tensions in Mosul were becoming incendiary. On 18 April, Petraeus received orders to transfer his division promptly. Thus for Petraeus and the soldiers of the 101st, their first order of business was to move from the areas near Baghdad where they had consolidated, to Mosul, in northern Iraq. Given its air assault capabilities and the long reach of its helicopters, the 101st was an ideal solution to an increasingly inflammatory situation.

To get to Mosul, Iraq's third-largest city and the provincial capital of Ninewa Province, about 250 miles north of Baghdad, the 101st conducted the longest air assault in the history of the U.S. Army. It was a successful mission and was the kind of operation for which they had long trained back in the United States, and one they would repeat in coming months in pursuit of insurgent fighters.

The ancient city of Mosul was a cauldron of boiling tensions. It was a place where long-standing ethnic and religious tensions simmered, fueled by deep and relentless animosities. It had once been an important trading center between Persia to the east and the Mediterranean lands to the west, and it was still the economic and political capital of Ninewa Province as well as a cultural center. It was a majority Sunni city but boasted a mixed population of about 2 million Sunnis, Shia, Kurds, Christians, and Turkomans. The Sunni hold was tenuous, and the large number of Kurds who lived there had long been restless, due in no small part to agitations arising from the proximity of the neighboring semiautonomous region of Kurdistan. Many Kurds harbored separatist aspirations and were seeking claims to the oil-rich area around the city of Kirkuk, the province of Ninewa other major urban center. With the fall of Hussein's regime, U.S. intelligence agencies grew concerned that if Kurdish interests—especially the military arm of the Kurds, the *peshmerga*—seized power, Turkey could directly intervene to halt them, and a new war would erupt.

When the 101st's advanced units reached Mosul on 22 April, they found a gloomy and daunting situation. There were no competent security forces in the city, and pillaging was widespread. Tens of thousands of Iraqi army troops were in the vicinity, out of action and restless. *Peshmerga* had indeed been in the city, where they stole what Iraqi military supplies and weapons they could find, to include some U.S. supplies that had been placed there without sufficient protection. The *peshmerga* remained in the area and had apparently retreated to assemble in the nearby hills. The local police force had fled in fear and disarray after they were attacked and their stations looted. Not even their vehicles remained. On the west side of town, skirmishing continued between Arab factions. Its specific cause was unknown, but any number of scores were likely being settled in the absence of any authority. A thick pall hung over the area from burning ammunition and building fires that sprouted throughout the city. Nobody tried to extinguish them. Mosul's residents were hunkered out of sight, without electricity, fresh water, or regular sources of food. Local government was completely broken down. U.S. forces consisted mostly of a contingent of marines, who were concentrated around the airport.

Petraeus sent the first 1,600 troops who air-assaulted to the city center to show an overwhelming military presence and begin to demonstrate that the United States intended to restore security. Soon the division's helicopters filled the sky, and sounds of their blades could be heard whomping at all hours. He was not trying to act as an imperial occupier, but to establish order. Petraeus gave directions to the division to be visible, but not aggressive; to treat local residents with respect, but to act decisively against anyone who committed violence. He modeled confidence himself—removing his Kevlar helmet and flak jacket whenever possible during foot tours through city neighborhoods and when speaking with Iraqis. He abandoned the customary U.S. practice of *cordon and sweep* operations, in which U.S. troops establish a perimeter and round up all of the military-age males within it, as counterproductive. He concluded that family privacy, a powerful virtue in Arabic society, meant that many Iraqi men, even those who were actively opposing the United States, would voluntarily surrender if cornered rather than subject their families to searches within their homes in the middle of the night. These were the first steps to restoring the confidence of the population. But Petraeus faced enormous obstacles. Neither he nor his division really understood the dynamics on the ground. It was nearly impossible to differentiate the agendas of the many factions contesting for power and influence. There was just no way to tell a good guy from a bad guy.

Petraeus's mission in this complex environment, beyond establishing security, was to keep the peace, assure essential services to the population, and begin the process of rebuilding a civic society with a functioning local government. It was a herculean set of missions. The extensive list of unconventional problems confronting Petraeus in this environment was in no way part of the division's normal war-fighting tasks that they had trained to solve. Army doctrine traditionally assigned such duties to specially organized and prepared civil affairs units. But such troops were in critically short supply across the army, and not available to Petraeus. So he would have to make do with the troops he had. And he needed to act quickly, before events spun out of control in Mosul.

Petraeus's troops were the only viable, non-Iraqi organization in northern Iraq capable of addressing Mosul's extraordinary range of challenges. Neither civilian relief and aid organizations, referred to as nongovernmental Agencies, or NGOs, nor the United Nations, had more than a handful of people on the ground and only the most limited capacity to operate. What the 101st possessed were the things in most urgent need to begin to fill the vacuum of government: trained and responsive man-power, top-quality communications equipment, mobility on the ground and in the air, and superior planning and leadership abilities. But these assets would have to be applied in novel ways if Petraeus was to achieve success. It wouldn't be enough just to have superior technology, wealth, and the overwhelming firepower. Rather, the key, as Petraeus knew, was for his soldiers to quickly—very quickly—adapt to their new and unfa-miliar environment. They must learn that their job was to keep the citi-zenry safe while they restored basic services and gave the Iraqis time to rebuild their society. Iraqis would have to be made to feel that they had a real part to play in the new Iraq that was being built. And the soldiers must be sure that U.S. actions on the ground did not create any new enemies.

One test case for Petraeus's ability to convince Iraqis of the good in-tentions of U.S. soldiers came later in the summer. Iraqis quickly noted the ubiquitous night-vision devices donned by soldiers that allowed U.S. troops to operate successfully at night. The power of this technol-ogy seemed boundless, and rumors soon spread that, in fact, soldiers were using the devices to see through women's clothing. Clearly, if true, this was a grave affront and local speculation led to much agitation in the city. When the division's commanders heard of this, they responded in unique fashion. To demonstrate that night-vision devices only amplify light waves not visible to the naked eye but do not in any way penetrate solid objects, including clothing, they called a meeting of sheikhs and tribal leaders. At the meeting, soldiers demonstrated how the devices worked and allowed the Iraqis to try them out. Satisfied that the technology did not violate the dignity of their families, the meeting grew into a forum for solving other contentious issues.

Petraeus also took the novel step of reorganizing the division, starting with key staff functions, to better align with existing Iraqi governmen-tal structures. Some of the alignments were obvious: the 101st's division surgeon and medical team were assigned to work with the Iraqi Ministry of Health. The staff communications experts were paired with the Tele-communications Ministry; and the division engineers, with the Ministry of Public Works. In some cases, there were civic responsibilities that were so different from traditional military functions that he simply had to as-sign manpower to the problem and trust the leadership and ingenuity of his soldiers to improvise solutions. Hence the division aviation brigade, in addition to flying their helicopters, would also support the students and faculty of Mosul University. The university had been closed due to the violence, and Petraeus wanted it reopened as soon as possible. Likewise, the division support command would sustain the 101st with supply and transportation, and they would also help Iraqi officials from the Ministries of Education and Youth and Sports.

Petraeus also ensured that there was only one boss in charge of the region—him. He established a joint task force that included all U.S. government personnel in the operating area and directed them to keep him informed of their activities. In everything, Petraeus communicated consistently and relentlessly. Daily command briefings became a stage upon which he could reinforce his strategic vision. And he made it clear that he was going to implement the lessons he had been studying throughout his professional life about irregular warfare. When asked what he considered to be the central lesson of counterinsurgency operations, Petraeus replied crisply: "Secure the population."[1]

Looking back on these weeks much later, Petraeus described his approach:

> [Regarding Mosul with 101st . . . ,] it was very clear early on that we, the military, were going to have to do the nation building. People occasionally ask, "What were the big decisions you made in Iraq?" The biggest decision I made early on in Iraq that I announced—to a little bit of stunned silence from the commanders—was that we [were] going to do nation building.[2]

In all that he did, Petraeus promoted his vision that reconstruction would have to be from the ground up, rather than the top-down measures typically favored by Western nations in the aftermath of conflict, and currently in favor in Washington. As Petraeus later commented:

> What you do is get a general concept, you get some organizing principles, you explain it all as clearly as you can, and then you unleash the productivity of the people, if you will, our people and then their people, and get on with it because there was an enormous capability in the Iraqis as well. There were thousands of trained, certified

engineers, just in northern Iraq alone. There is a huge legal community. There is a huge educated class and so forth. It was just a matter of getting them going again, engaged and enabled somewhat
with resources, because of course the [national] ministries weren't
yet doing that.[3]

Unfortunately, Petraeus found himself largely without any additional
support or resources in these endeavors and, in many respects, hampered
by broader U.S. policy in Iraq. Initially, the senior agent for implementing U.S. policy in Iraq was the Office for Reconstruction and Humanitarian Assistance (OHRA), established in January by the United States to
provide a governmental framework for Iraq in the immediate aftermath
of the expected American invasion. It was led by retired lieutenant general Jay Garner, but Garner was dismissed after Baghdad fell in the wake
of disputes between him and authorities in Washington. Responsibility
for policy then shifted to OHRA's successor, the Coalition Provisional
Authority, or CPA. Its precise legal origins were vague, but by May, the
United States and the United Kingdom as chief allies in the Coalition,
had created the CPA to be the transitional government for Iraq. President Bush appointed Ambassador L. Paul Bremer III as its head on 11 May.
Over the coming months, the CPA cited UN Security Resolution 1483
for its legitimacy. This resolution was vested in Chapter VII of the UN
Charter and the customary laws of war to grant broad authority to Coali-
tion forces for the welfare of the Iraqi people. Thus, the basic role of the
CPA as it evolved was to administer Iraq until its full sovereignty could
be restored. All of the military commanders in Iraq thus depended on the
CPA for guidance concerning all matters of reconstruction.

One of the most central tasks facing Petraeus was the lack of any co-
herent government, either in Mosul or in the province. Hence, he decided to hold elections and to do so right away. Before Garner departed,
Petraeus had spoken to Garner and was given permission to hold elections, but Petraeus didn't wait for detailed instructions, not from Washington, nor from U.S. officials in Baghdad. So his first step was to call a
meeting of several dozen prominent Iraqis—businessmen, former generals, sheikhs, politicians, and lawyers, both Arab and Kurds, to a meeting
in what had been a Baath Party reception hall. It wasn't at all clear ex-
actly who was present at the meeting. While the Iraqis knew each other,

their relative stations weren't apparent to Petraeus and the small group of division officers who tried to bring order to the session. Only when the Iraqis seated themselves did the Americans somewhat divine how at least the Iraqis saw themselves—the important figures were seated at the front and in the better chairs, the lesser persons further back.

Petraeus opened the forum by reminding the group that the Americans, and by that he meant himself especially, were in charge. He admonished them that violence would not be tolerated and that all those who sought to disrupt the creation of a new civic community for Mosul would be punished. He then proposed an electoral process that would allocate delegates to elect an interim provincial council and governor according to the region's tribes and political parties. Each group would be allotted representatives in proportion to their population. This concept was sound, but neither Petraeus nor the Iraqis had any firm idea of population totals, and each group immediately exaggerated their own numbers and diminished those of their opponents. On a few earlier occasions, he had tried to explain to the Iraqis that the wonder of representative government was that all had the opportunity to register their opinions and positions. It was by design an inclusive and rambunctious process, but one that must be engaged in while retaining respect for the opposition. But emotions were too raw, and the Iraqis too splintered for lectures in civic affairs. As the crescendo of argument rose, Petraeus shouted, "Stop!" He insisted that he would abandon the entire process if the Iraqis did not begin to cooperate. They did, and a week later returned with a negotiated settlement for an election.

Several days later, the nominated delegates assembled to conduct the election. As Petraeus pointed out to the group: "By being here today you are participating in the birth of the democratic process in Iraq. . . . This is a historic occasion and an important step forward for Mosul and Iraq."[4] And indeed it was. For the first time since Saddam Hussein had come to power decades previously, Iraqis were participating in an election without any coercion. Nowhere else in Iraq was this happening. By noon, the balloting was complete for the council. Its 24 members represented each of Ninewa's various groups and parties: Kurds, Sunnis, Shiites, Turkomans, Assyrians, Yezidis, Christians, and even some former Baath Party members were seated. And several hours later, the governor was elected. He was Ghanim al-Basso, a retired general and former

Baathist before being arrested and having his brother killed by Hussein. Al-Basso was a bit of a known quantity, possessed some experience, and was considered trustworthy. It was important for the Iraqis to have their own political leader, even an interim one, at this stage. The election had not been ideal, but it had worked. As Petraeus complimented the crowd of delegates for their accomplishment, he sought to build a bridge between them and himself. "Having walked the streets of this city, the second largest in Iraq, and having gotten to know the friendly nature of its citizens, I am beginning to feel like a Moslawi," he stated.[5] It was a confident pronouncement.

Proud of what the 101st had achieved, Petraeus directed his staff to create a briefing that outlined the process he had pioneered. He assumed that the other American units in Iraq would now proceed to also hold elections in the same manner. But his fellow commanders each had different priorities. Conditions across Iraq were unique to each region, and the other army divisions were working on different timelines with different levels of violence and local expectations. And none of them had Petraeus's insights into the necessity of establishing political systems to bind the population to their own leaders. And from Washington came a sign that different calculations were in play as well. There would be no further regional elections because U.S. senior officials feared that fundamentalists might win any future runoff since radicals were gaining strength and organizing, especially in Baghdad's mosques.

But then, on the heels of the successful, although exceedingly delicate, balance Petraeus had achieved in the north, two blows to his aspirations for Mosul came from Baghdad. These shocks weren't from Iraqis or insurgents, but from America's administrator of Iraq, Ambassador Bremer, now leading the CPA.

In May 2003, Bremer issued two orders that would have far-reaching consequences for Iraq. The first outlawed the Baath Party and prohibited most of those who had been members from serving in the new Iraqi government. The second dissolved Iraq's armed forces and security forces. Together, the two orders destabilized the nascent progress underway to rebuild Iraq's political process because they caused the loss of many civil service professionals just at the moment when their experience was most needed.

To Petraeus and other observant leaders on the ground, these directives were shortsighted. It seemed that officials in Washington were comparing postinvasion Iraq with the conditions that existed in Germany during the months and years following World War II, but it was sheer folly to compare the two, given the varied historical differences. In Germany, there had been a unified cultural tradition that the overwhelming majority of individual Germans shared. Common religious beliefs and political traditions stretching back centuries had created a mostly homogeneous society that even the tribulations of war and the seizure of the nation by the Nazis with their twisted ideology, could not eradicate. In contrast, Iraq was not only new as a nation-state, having been demarcated by Western powers as a consequence of the settlement of World War I and the final dissolution of the Ottoman Empire, it was also riven by crosscutting ethnic and tribal rivalries, and was partitioned by the Sunni-Shia schism.

The demarcation between Sunni and Shia, which long characterized contemporary Islam, also fueled so much of the sectarian animosity in Iraq. This tension dates to disputes that erupted within the faith shortly after the death of Islam's founder, the Prophet Muhammad, in A.D. 632, Sunnis, whose name comes from the Arabic term meaning "one who follows the traditions of the Prophet," support the principle that the leader of Islam should be elected from those with the most capability to safeguard the faithful. Shias (from *Shia-t-Ali*, or "the Party of Ali") think that the leader should have been a member of Muhammad's family or someone personally chosen by him. Hence, Sunnis advocate that the man chosen, Muhammad's close friend and advisor, Abu Bakr, was the proper choice, while Shias see this as an error, instead favoring Muhammad's cousin and son-in-law, Ali. From this first question of political succession, a number of divergences in spiritual theology and practice evolved, so that over time, the two groups became quite distinct communities that have wrestled for dominance for many centuries.

Iraqis' sense of nationalism, while powerful, had to contest with this longstanding religious competition as well as with matters of individual clan membership for their loyalty. Hence the prospect that Iraq would be able to quickly heal and a new, consensus government would arise was a wish that Iraqis themselves well knew to be naive. Under Hussein, the

Baathist Party had exploited the fractures of Iraqi society, and now that society would not likely heal easily.

The Baathist Party, whose name means "rebirth," was established in 1947 in Syria. Baathists opposed continued Western European imperialism and sought to reduce European influences in the Middle East. It was a part of the broader rebirth of Arab nationalism across the region that witnessed the reassertion of local rule as Europeans retreated. Unfortunately, many of the newly founded governments proved to be despotic. Such was the case in Iraq. To increase his control, Hussein gradually militarized and centralized the party, relying upon cells at the local village level who reported to regional committees led by his cronies. To reward them for their loyalty, Hussein exchanged the information they could provide for steady jobs and access to housing, automobiles, health care, education, and consumer goods unavailable to those outside the party. Party rosters eventually numbered several million, but it was only those near the top of the party's hierarchy who controlled the political and economic life of Iraq. While it was true that many Iraqis had been willing members of Hussein's ruling Baathist Party, Petraeus knew full well that many tens of thousands of others had been compelled to identify with the Baathists to protect themselves and their families.

As Petraeus commented, "We always tried to make a distinction between the Saddamists and those that were in the Baath Party . . . down the food chain, as a way of getting a job or an education." He noted that, "Many of those Sunnis who were cast out were Western-educated. They were really the ones that we wanted to have help run the country; they actually understood how the country ran; they spoke English; they were much more secular, in most cases. And then not only did we lose them, we actually, in many cases, thrust some of them into the insurgent camp because their entire incentive was to oppose the new Iraq, not to support it. Ending an insurgency or keeping one from starting involves trying to give as many people as possible a stake in the success of the new Iraq."[6]

These key points were not initially understood in Washington, but essential to the revival of Iraq. Most of the middle tier of Iraq's professional and technical classes—government workers, professors, scientists, engineers, pilots, and even police and military leaders—were Baathists in name only. These men and women were desperately needed to revive the economy now. The senior members of the Baathist Party who bore enough criminal guilt to bear prosecution were the ones in hiding or had already fled to other countries. In any case, they were not seeking to join the new government.

In response to these criticisms that erupted after the orders were issued, CPA officials countered that Baathists who had held high-ranking positions could not be trusted. These ex-party members would likely seek to topple the new government and restore some kind of autocratic rule. There was also the matter of justice. Those Iraqis who had been harmed during Hussein's rule deserved to see a new government fully purged of Baathist influence. The CPA especially pointed to Petraeus and the elections he had orchestrated as a fresh problem. CPA officials held that several provincial council members, including Governor Basso, should be removed from office. Their ousters would, of course, upset the delicate political balance operating in Mosul, so Petraeus requested reconsideration. He didn't make a big case of the situation publicly, he simply adopted a broad interpretation of the CPA's intent and sought ways to circumvent it quietly. Such was the case of Mosul University.

Bremer's order applied to the removal of the majority of the school's faculty, who were struggling to revive the institution. Since educational opportunity, and the gainful employment of the faculty, were twin goals of Petraeus's reconstruction programs, he sought an alternative. Turning to his legal team on the division staff, they located text in the Geneva Conventions, the internationally sanctioned treaties and protocols that specified the treatment of civilians in wartime, that demanded occupying powers guarantee civil institutions devoted to children's education be sustained. Bremer conceded Petraeus's point, allowing the faculty to be fired and then immediately rehired on a temporary basis as part of a local reconciliation gesture in Mosul. And he allowed Petraeus to support a panel of Iraqis in Mosul to conduct a Reconciliation Commission, as he came to recognize the importance of reconciling many of the tens of thousands of former midlevel Baathists who were thrown out of work and left with no incentive to support the new Iraq. Unfortunately, it was an accommodation that was ultimately short lived. Bremer had given responsibility for the implementation of the de-Baathification edict to a national committee, and this body opposed Petraeus's plans. Petraeus protested to the Pentagon, but to little avail. Too many White House aides and policy officials supported the program, and in Iraq, Ahmed

Chalabi, a Shia political broker who would prove to have multiple political loyalties in the service of his outsized ambitions, headed the commission and blocked most reconciliation proposals. The result was a loss of
faith among Sunnis in northern Iraq that they could find a constructive
place in the new government. Their dissatisfaction turned for some into
outright resistance, fueling a growing resistance movement and undermining the CPA's ambitions of a stable Iraq.

The second CPA order, disbanding Iraq's half-million man armed
forces and intelligence bureaus, also hit hard in Mosul. By this directive,
former military officers in the rank of colonel or above could join Iraq's
new security services only after extensive vetting. Despite its excesses
during Hussein's reign, the army was a unifying force for Iraq and a source
of income for the rank and file at a moment when the economy was in
tatters. This order disenfranchised hundreds of thousands of men, literally turning them into the streets when U.S. leaders most needed them
working. Protests erupted across Iraq. In Mosul, more than a dozen soldiers were wounded in attacks prompted by the U.S. orders. Petraeus told
the CPA in Baghdad that American soldiers were now at heightened risk.
In June, former soldiers who had lost their pensions, and a fair measure
of their dignity, attacked Mosul's city hall. In response, the frightened
police and security personnel on duty returned fire, killing one protestor.
Vehicles were torched, and it looked for a time as if the entire building
would be plundered. Petraeus personally intervened, ultimately calming
the crowd and offering to host a meeting between him, Governor Basso,
and the ringleaders to listen to their grievances. Soon after, the governor
and Petraeus approved the banning of public demonstrations until the
situation could be righted, but this was only a temporary measure that
didn't address the underlying causes of the public's discontent. More was
needed to address their grievances.

These men, many of whom were veterans of the long and bloody Iraq-
Iran war of the 1980s, believed that they had served their country honor-
ably and were entitled to their retirement payments and had nothing for
which to apologize. The vast majority already denounced Hussein's tyranny and felt their personal participation in the armed forces a matter of
national duty. In the fall, in what Petraeus later described with a smile as
"a wild scheme," he initiated Baath Party renunciation ceremonies. Their
purpose was to provide former Baathists and service members a process

that would inspire confidence in their future in Iraq. During these events, large crowds, sometimes numbering more than 2,000, gathered to try to find a way to restore their place in society. During one session, Petraeus greeted the attendees personally. "The individuals gathered here have assembled voluntarily," he intoned to onlookers. "Their only benefit will be the sense of personal closure that comes from disavowing links with the former regime and supporting those who are building the new Iraq."[7] Each Iraqi was given the opportunity to sign a declaration renouncing their former ties to the Baathist forces and take vows embracing the new government. Here and throughout the city, Petraeus ordered U.S. forces to treat former regime officers (other than unreconciled Hussein supporters) with professional dignity, as another small sign that America wanted reconciliation for all Iraqis.

Petraeus took other steps also. He worked behind the scenes to bolster Basso's grip in office, which was always tenuous given the strains the governor was under and the fragmented support he drew from the populace. Petraeus also met with a local retired officers association, originally orchestrated by U.S. Special Forces troops in the area but now also being assisted by the 101st. Petraeus knew that such organizations had the potential to provide the means for these unhappy former soldiers to air their complaints and for the 101st to offer them opportunities for reintegration. But as with other similar programs, the CPA's resistance and the indifference by the Iraqi national government in the capital city meant that Petraeus was confined to local solutions with limited reach, and ultimately, limited success. What was missing was a nationwide reconciliation program orchestrated from Baghdad. No such program would be established until Petraeus took command of Multi-National Force Iraq (MNF-I) in 2007.

In the spring of 2004, it was clear even to Bremer and the CPA that de-Baathification was a failed initiative. In April Bremer announced that it had been "poorly implemented" and applied "unevenly and unjustly" and said that he supported a plan to allow "vetted senior officers from the former regime" back into the military services. A CPA spokesman emphasized that Baathists "who do not have blood on their hands" and who were "innocent and competent" could play a role in Iraq's reconstruction.[8] Two months later, Bremer dissolved the Supreme National de-Baathification Commission, and interim Iraqi prime minister Ayad

Allawi backed the return of vetted ex-Baathists to the security services after his appointment in June 2004. But by then, Petraeus and the 101st had already departed, a full-fledged insurgency was gaining momentum, and Iraq was falling into chaos.

NOTES

1. Fareed Zakaria, "The General: An Interview with David Petraeus, the Head of Central Command and the Commander of Iraq during the Bush Siege," *Newsweek,* December 28, 2009, http://www.newsweek.com/2009/01/03/the-general.html.

2. Ibid.

3. Donald Wright and Timothy Reese, *On Point II* (Ft. Leavenworth, KS: Combat Studies Institute Press, 2008), 129.

4. Cloud and Jaffe, *The Fourth Star,* 120.

5. Ibid., 120–21.

6. Zakaria, "The General," http://www.newsweek.com/2009/01/03/the-general.html.

7. Cloud and Jaffe, *The Fourth Star,* 140–41.

8. Sharon Otterman, "Iraq: Debaathification," *Council on Foreign Relations,* April 7, 2005, http://www.cfr.org/publication/7853/iraq.html.

Chapter 13

THE WAR IN NORTHERN IRAQ AND BEYOND

Petraeus's success in Mosul over the course of 2003 drew increasing attention from the American media and political class. Ever savvy to public affairs, Petraeus made the most of the opportunity to tell the 101st's story. For years, Petraeus had groomed himself to be a master at communication, and his skills came into full flower while commanding in northern Iraq. Petraeus became brilliant at harnessing the stagecraft essential to effective leadership. He relished the semiautonomous role that in part had resulted by happenstance and in part he had carved for himself. Now he used the opportunity of being in charge and far from Baghdad to the utmost. Unlike in many army units, where visitors are largely treated as unwelcome interlopers, Petraeus's personal staff extended a warm welcome and were inevitably solicitous. Official guests were hosted in the Ninewa Hotel, a former Baathist retreat that Petraeus convinced the provincial council to privatize and turn into a business to generate income. Governor Basso typically made an appearance to reinforce Petraeus's narrative and to put an important Iraqi face on America's reconstruction efforts.

Petraeus kept up a vigorous personal training regime. After waking to a quick 20 minutes of reading overnight reports and replying to critical e-mails, he started each day with a run, often extending to five miles around the base with members of his personal staff. Next, he conducted the morning's first formal event for the division's leadership, the daily battle update. Petraeus led this and every meeting with a purpose. He was the master of details, wielding his authority through information dominance. His briefings were well-crafted theater, a combination of instruction, encouragement, and communication. He took a seat at the center of the front row, his staff perched behind tiered rows of desks behind him, all staring at large screens on which the army's ubiquitous slides, created by Microsoft's PowerPoint software, were flashed. It was like a slow-motion film, with Petraeus starting and stopping each scene with a curt, "got it," "ok," "roger," or "go ahead." He invariably opened these briefings with a sharp, "This is Eagle Six" and with a touch of mirth, "It's another beautiful morning in the Tigris Valley."[1]

Holding a laser pointer in one hand, and occasionally fondling a microphone with the other, Petraeus would orchestrate the hour-long command performances. Like much of what Petraeus pioneered in northern Iraq, these briefings over the subsequent years became de rigueur in Iraq. Every command, of course, conducted daily updates, but few initially featured the level of detail that Petraeus demanded on a daily basis. Issues were deliberately wide ranging, and Petraeus peppered individual staff officers with questions. Security concerns always topped the list, but by no means were they the only, nor sometimes the most urgent, issue of the day. Activity at local markets, health and sanitation improvements, government office reconstruction, performance of private contractors, highway improvements, and the ever-important oil sector of the economy were each discussed in turn; and because he kept a sharp eye on the media, the public affairs staff brought to Petraeus's attention the prominent publications appearing in the press, both in the region and back in the United States. And of course, as such meetings drew to a close, Petraeus could be counted on to emphasize, as a slide flashed on screen, the ethos he was learning to cultivate in himself and others, "We are in a race to win over the people. What have you and your element done today?"[2]

Only selected outsiders witnessed these updates, but the ones who were accorded the privilege were those who could influence decisions in Washington. Petraeus himself typically made time for important delegations, receiving them in his large upstairs office that like many of Iraq's official residences used during Saddam Hussein's time, featured lattice-work ceilings, warmly painted colors, marble tiling, and in this case, a view of the Tigris River in the background. A broader group was given the opportunity to watch a short video produced by the 101st illustrating the division's accomplishments. Troops were seen cleaning up streets, speaking with locals, chasing down insurgents, and generally restoring order in Mosul. The video concluded with a scene of Petraeus memorializing a fallen battalion commander while a bagpiper played "Amazing Grace." "There is nothing tougher than the loss of a brother in arms," he solemnly declared. "We want to find meaning and purpose in such a loss. Above all we want to answer the question: What good will come from this?" The video concluded with a famous image of World War II troops from the 101st posing with a captured Nazi flag. The grainy image of the proud but tired men clutching their war trophy then faded into a photo of contemporary Screaming Eagles presenting an Iraqi flag amid city ruins in a similar pose. It wasn't a Hollywood production, but it was sincere, even if quite clearly earnest. And when shown to visitors who had already been treated to a briefing by Petraeus, interviews with soldiers, and tours of the latest U.S. equipment—all set amid Hussein's former palaces, most of which were typically decorated with themes of Arab warriors—the experience was evocative.

In November, Petraeus summarized to an interviewer the path that he had taken with the 101st so far:

The first thing we needed to do was re-establish some degree of security and start rebuilding respect for the law—and a culture, if you will, of law and order—because that had totally broken down. There were private armies roaming the streets. There were political leaders who were proclaiming themselves to be the governor and mayor and all the other officials. All the government buildings had been looted. The looting was still continuing, and basic law-and-order policing was just non-existent. So that was the very first job.

We managed to do that fairly quickly by just flat blanketing Mosul itself with four infantry battalions, an Apache attack helicopter battalion, a tank battalion, an artillery battalion, a light

attack helicopter OH58 battalion, and so forth. We started getting security under control.

Then we realized that, in addition to just getting basic services
restored and getting businesses, shops, schools and universities reopened, the other thing that we needed to address was this incredible power vacuum that existed really all the way from Baghdad
down to the district and sub-district level. So we took that on.[3]

Petraeus was increasingly driving home to his soldiers the point that
in addition to establishing political stability, they must create greater
economic opportunity for Iraqis. As he explained at the time:

Unemployment's a big problem, because if people aren't getting a
paycheck, they don't see a stake in the new Iraq . . . So why should
they support this grand new experiment that's unfolding around
them? . . . Now, they'll never starve, of course. There's a tremendous social safety network in place here in Iraq that remains. There's
food distribution that goes on, so they won't starve. There is medical care which is reasonably good in this region. So their very basic
needs will be taken care of. They're not charged for electricity,
they're not charged for water, they're not charged for most things.
But they don't have jobs, and they don't feel like they're doing
something productive; they're not advancing themselves. All they're
doing is surviving. Again, you've got to do much more than survive if you're going to throw your hand in fully with the new Iraq.[4]

However, security conditions, which had seemed to be on a positive
trajectory in the spring and summer, were now stalling. Then tragedy
struck in mid-November when 17 U.S. soldiers were killed when two
Blackhawk helicopters collided over Mosul. Remembering the incident later, Petraeus said, "The loss of 17 soldiers in one night when two
helicopters collided over Mosul was just a blow beyond belief," he said.
"It's like losing 17 children. It's almost beyond comprehension—a terrible, terrible blow to the organization and the individuals in it." The
mooring following this loss, a young trooper from the headquarters staff
approached the commanding general. "Sir," he began, "That just gives
us 17 more reasons to get this right." Petraeus looked hard at the soldier

and, in the following weeks, repeated those words. "I drew an awful lot of strength from that particular soldier that morning," Petraeus later admitted.[5]

So the 101st kept up the pressure on the insurgents. By Thanksgiving, the division had captured 190 AK-47s, machine guns, and pistols; 65 rocket propelled grenade (RPG) rounds; 40 RPG launchers; 130 grenades; 80,000 rounds of ammunition; 470 mortar rounds; 116 rockets; and 11 antitank missiles. U.S. troops solicited local Iraqis to help, with some success. The same month that violence overall against the 101st was higher than it had been, about 800 RPG rounds, 500 RPG launchers, almost 2,000 hand grenades, and several dozen surface-to-air missiles had been turned in by the populace. Hundreds of items used in the construction of improvised explosive devices (IEDs), such as detonators, wiring, timers, and explosives, were also handed over to the Americans.

Jump-starting the local economy, especially while security conditions remained tenuous, was costly. The division would eventually receive a share of the $20 billion in reconstruction funds approved by the U.S. Congress, but those monies had not yet arrived. In the meantime, the 101st had nearly spent the approximately $30 million of confiscated Baath Party funds provided by the CPA, including some taken from the safe house where Uday and Qusay Hussein had been killed several months previously. The 101st had played the key role in that incident also.

In late July, soldiers from the 101st, along with members of Task Force 20, the joint military unit dedicated to finding and capturing or killing the key leaders of the Baathist regime, surrounded Uday and Qusay Hussein, Saddam's notorious sons, in a residence in Mosul. Like their fugitive father, they had remained on the run. Uday was the ace of hearts, and Qusay was the ace of clubs on the famous deck of playing cards publicized by the Coalition as a modern form of a most-wanted roster. Both were wanted for the many crimes they had committed against their fellow Iraqis, including assault, robbery, theft, and murder. When an Iraqi tipster indicated to 101st troops that the pair were nearby, Task Force 20 and the 101st moved in, isolating the suspected hideout. Soldiers from the 101st established a security perimeter, and soon a gunfight broke out when special operations forces conducted an initial assault. For awhile, fire from the barricaded brothers was intense, but a barrage of vehicle-mounted TOWs (wire guided missiles) fired by the 101st severely damaged the building and sealed the fate of those inside. When U.S. forces finally entered several hours later, they found both brothers already dead. It was another high point for the Americans, and a further blow to those Baathists who were still holding out faint dreams of a reconquest.

Saddam Hussein himself was eluding U.S. forces, but his time as a free man was running out too as his Coalition pursuers were tightening their noose. Drawing upon a network of still-loyal followers to protect him, he managed to evade capture until December when soldiers found him cowering in a small underground cellar. His detention put a certain dagger into any fanciful notions of a Baathist resurgence and was portrayed by American generals and political leaders alike as vindication of the U.S. invasion and a moment of triumph.

With Hussein and the remaining senior Baathists dead, captured, or in hiding, and with a new government up and running in Ninewa Province, what Petraeus wanted to do most was to energize the economy. He pushed his commanders to spend all available resources, in an approach that when later formalized was known as the Commanders' Emergency Response Program (CERP). The intent of CERP was to give U.S. military leaders in Iraq the ability to distribute money rapidly and efficiently to fund relatively small projects. Its bureaucratic requirements were lessened so that the red tape normally associated with reconstruction projects could be avoided. Over time, CERP proved to be a tremendous success. But Petraeus knew that CERP cash wouldn't be enough to get the economy humming. It cost more money than the 101st would ever have to pay the salaries of government workers, outfit the newly hired police, stand up a court system, and build medical facilities and schools. Thus, he sought ways to accelerate trade and business so that the Iraqis could begin funding their own requirements. By increasing the supply (or manufacture) of goods, Iraqis would see that their quality of life was improving, inflation would be brought under control, and more business owners could find gainful opportunity.

Casting about for something decisive, Petraeus hit upon the idea of opening the border with Iraq's neighbor to the west, Syria. As had been the case when he decided to hold elections, the extent of his authority was not precisely clear. But UN resolutions governing trade with Iraq were expansive enough to permit some latitude. So once again, he huddled with the lawyer on his staff and concluded that there existed an "emergency to remain in effect" that condoned opening border traffic, and any such arrangement would remain operative "until revoked by a higher authority."[6] Having decreed this, several days later, he and Governor Basso boarded helicopters for the flight to the small, barren outpost of Rabiya to hold a small ceremony marking the opening of the crossing there.

Before a crowd of hundreds of sheikhs who had hastily assembled (there would be nearly a thousand at the postceremony gathering), Petraeus spoke a few words extolling the gains to be obtained from increased commerce between Iraq and Syria. One of the most important products that would transit the border was oil. Petraeus's staff had been negotiating with Syrian officials who had visited Mosul using Petraeus's own helicopters to sell them Iraqi crude in exchange for electricity, which was urgently needed in the region. Since the animosity between the Syrians and Iraqis was so great, American commanders served as intermediaries as negotiations haltingly proceeded. At one point, the Syrians insisted that they must have approval of their superiors in Damascus before a deal could be done, but Petraeus convinced them that immediate resolution was in everyone's best interest. He hinted that if the Syrians took their concerns to Damascus, they would likely see fewer profits for themselves. It worked, and hence, Petraeus was now at the border, watching the senior Iraqi and Syrian minister in the area symbolically turn the valve signaling the resumption of oil flowing westward. To seal the deal, a goat was sacrificed, each side dipping their hands in the flowing blood and laying hands on the pipeline. Neither Baghdad nor Damascus subsequently overturned the arrangement. Some later said that Petraeus was thus the only division commander in the army with his own foreign policy.

Petraeus worked other incentives on behalf of the Iraqis too. To pay for upgrades to border facilities and to provide an incentive for border guards to facilitate trade, he coordinated for an administrative fee to be paid for each truck that crossed. No doubt the guards skimmed some of the fees, but if the result was more trade, then it was worth it. Such was the cultural practice in the region, and Petraeus needed business to get done. Legal reform would follow, in time. The 101st's staff made a similar arrangement with Turkish businessmen. Turkey too could provide electricity in exchange for Iraqi oil. Bit by bit, the economy revived, but thorough political reconciliation, which would have allowed a full revival of commercial activity, remained elusive.

A particularly thorny problem was the nagging dilemma posed by the Kurds. The Kurds are a non-Arabic people who are largely Sunni Muslims and speak a language related to Persian. They number more than 20 million in the region and live in the mountainous areas that straddle the territory of modern-day Iraq, Syria, Iran, and Turkey. When the Ottoman Empire broke apart after World War I, the Kurds sought a separate Kurdistan homeland, but the European powers ignored their plight. As has been the case for most of their history, they continued to be dominated by their more powerful neighbors. They have attempted to establish an independent state but have been defeated each time. During the late 1980s, Iraqis used chemical weapons against the Kurds, slaughtering thousands of men, women, and children. Several million Kurds fled Iraq, mostly to Iran, but some 5 million remain, about 17 percent of Iraq's total population. Notably, in the months after the American victory in the Persian Gulf War in 1991, the Kurds attempted again to assert their sovereignty but were severely attacked and punished by Hussein's army.

After the United States created a safe haven for the Kurds within Iraq by imposing a no-fly zone that denied Hussein the ability to use aircraft north of the 36th parallel, the Kurds have generally considered the United States to be a friend. As the insurgency mounted within Iraq in 2003 and after, the Kurds maintained order in the areas they controlled. However, the major source of tension between Kurds and Iraqis remained a serious source of concern, and a potential flash point. Petraeus repeatedly reminded the Kurds that they were a part of the new Iraq and hence must fly the official Iraqi flag over their government building along with their region's banner. He stressed that all Iraqis, whatever their ethnic identity and religious faith, must give their professional civic allegiance to Baghdad. But the peoples of Iraq, whether Kurd, Arab, or a minority group, struggled to adopt the kind of pluralistic nationalism so familiar to Americans. To appease Petraeus, and to avoid his scorn, Kurdish officials ran the Iraqi flag up their flagpole when the American general was visiting, then often replaced it with their Kurdish banner when he departed. To Petraeus, the Kurds amounted to another significant challenge, one for the time being that was not leading to violence but that needed constant attention to keep it that way.

As the 101st's time in Iraq began to wind down, General Abizaid, commanding U.S. Central Command and responsible for all U.S. forces in the Middle East, traveled to northern Iraq to meet with Petraeus. Abizaid was one of the U.S. officers who fully understood the tensions in play across northern Iraqi. He had first served there in the wake of the Persian Gulf War, when he was ordered there to help protect Kurdish civilians from reprisals by the Iraqi security forces. This time, his purpose was to discuss replacing Petraeus's approximately 20,000 soldiers with a replacement force that was less than half of the 101st's size. Neither man was comfortable with conditions, but each was resigned to the political realities in the United States. The chief reason for cutting down forces was that there was little appetite in Washington for keeping a large presence in Iraq. There were too many competing demands for them in other places and for their return home. Hence, the number of troops needed to be reduced, and northern Iraq seemed to be a good place to begin. There was a sense of hope in the region that was not equaled in other parts of Iraq, so the logic ran; thus with Mosul on the right path, the risk to America's objectives there was lower. So rather than interpreting the calm as a rationale to retain the structures and force levels that Petraeus had in place, the reasoning led to the opposite course of action. It was Petraeus's success that largely created the conditions for a reduction.

In future years in Iraq, Petraeus would make the collection of data about the operations of the forces under his command and the performance of the Iraqi government, economy, and armed forces into a detailed and comprehensive art form. He would defeat many critics by responding with so much precise information that refutations, especially from somebody not living in Iraq, did not seem credible. He began this approach in Mosul. Petraeus's briefings became downright alluring in their precision, a credit to his leadership style that few could match. Of course, some mistook the briefing charts for actual reality, which was always messier and more uncertain than the reams of statistics suggested. So if Petraeus seemed to be promising more certitude than circumstances warranted, well, that too was part of the impression he wanted to present to maintain the 101st's momentum. And at the end of the day, Petraeus was always careful to caveat his progress. Those who later complained that the 101st was accomplishing less than promised in northern Iraq were free all along to draw their own conclusions.

As they prepared to depart Iraq, the 101st's staff continued to catalog many of the successes that had been achieved under their watch. They noted that by January 2004, the number of security incidents had dropped. Only an average of five *hostile contacts*, meaning attacks and bombings, were occurring in the division's area of responsibility. At the same time, there were on the order of two dozen meetings each day between military leaders and local Iraqi officials and managers concerning reconstruction and stability operations. In other words, military conflict had been successfully diminished, and constructive engagement was on the upswing.

While such statistics about Mosul under the 101st were accurate, they didn't paint a full picture. Beneath the surface, the long-standing tensions still fomented throughout the region. And so some of the successes carefully crafted by the 101st began to come unhinged toward the end of its time there. Governor Basso was forced out of office, and Mosul's police force fell apart after many were killed and their bodies deposited around the city as warnings to others. Increasing numbers of insurgents sought refuge in Mosul after fleeing from U.S. military operations in Fallujah, and American troops were not present in sufficient numbers to counter them. A real blow came with the assassination of the replacement governor, which led to a walkout of Sunni Provincial Council members and accelerated a deteriorating spiral. Further, reconstruction and development funding, already declining in the last months of Petraeus's time, dried up further. Hence, U.S. forces found themselves short on two counts: unable to combat the resurgent enemy fighters opposing them, and possessing too little money to advance projects needed to instill confidence in the population.

Despite these setbacks to the American effort on the heels of Petraeus's departure, there was a tremendous amount to commend. Even though the situation in Mosul remained troubled and turbulent, Petraeus's energy and initiative meant that a broad insurgency in northern Iraq failed to develop in the months following the U.S. invasion. Petraeus had kept one step ahead of the many adversaries who were already looking for ways to split apart—through violence—the tenuous accommodations in place among Mosul's contending groups. It may have been that enemy fighters simply chose to bide their time, but as long as Petraeus was in charge, they dared not show themselves in large numbers. Through force of will, creativity, and communication with his soldiers and with the Iraqis, Petraeus had held Mosul together for almost a year.

The 101st had shown how a division that had been trained in the classic army tradition of fighting high-intensity, conventional ground warfare could, through effective and decisive leadership, adapt to a new environment. For years, pundits had argued that the army should dedicate a sizeable portion of its force structure to the creation of large units that were purpose-built for stability and peacekeeping operations. The army had wisely resisted, noting that it needed to retain the flexibility to respond to any kind of conflict and that going from high intensity to low intensity was more achievable than trying to go the other way. While the army was still making mistakes in Iraq and still had much to learn, Petraeus had put in place a basic counterinsurgency campaign quickly and effectively and, in so doing, kept the lid on northern Iraq. His efforts demonstrated the direction the rest of the army should follow, and how it must institutionalize the kinds of changes he had implemented to optimize ground forces for this kind of operation.

Departing Iraq, Petraeus knew that he had done well. While securing Iraq, the 101st oversaw the completion of more than 5,000 projects, built or rebuilt more than 500 schools and dozens of medical clinics, cleared hundreds of kilometers of roads, permitted economic activity to return to the region, and of course, literally created government structures for Mosul and Ninewa Province. The division had spent nearly $60 million of reclaimed Baathist money for these improvements.

Characterizing the 101st's time in Mosul, Petraeus said, "Oftentimes we felt as if our soldiers had a rifle in one hand and a wrench in the other. We were fighting, but we were also rebuilding."[7] Back home at Fort Campbell, Petraeus described his feelings about his troops to a grateful community:

The initiative by our young leaders and Soldiers is incredible, and we applaud it and encourage it. Half the time they're way out ahead of us, and that's where they ought to be. That's the American way.

The innovativeness of our Soldiers is extraordinary—their determination to do what they did in 125-degree heat during the summer when we were really in pretty primitive conditions; their courage to continue doing it as they're getting shot at and ambushed and improvised explosives detonated around their convoys. It's incredible. Again, the American public should be very, very proud of what our young Soldiers are doing out here.[8]

For his leadership, Petraeus would soon receive a third star. However, instead of returning to Fort Bragg to command, which seemed to be a likely and welcome assignment, he instead soon found himself once again in Iraq, this time leading the U.S. effort to rebuild Iraq's armed forces. It would prove a difficult endeavor, and one battered by the political narratives of American domestic affairs.

NOTES

1. Cloud and Jaffe, *The Fourth Star*, 130.

2. Ibid., 138.

3. Martin Smith, "Beyond Baghdad: Interview with General David Petraeus," *PBS Frontline*, November 23, 2003, http://www.pbs.org/wgbh/pages/frontline/shows/beyond/iraqis/nation.html.

4. Ibid.

5. Donna Miles, "Maj. Gen. David H. Petraeus Cites Highs and Lows of Iraqi Deployment," *American Forces Press Service*, March 17, 2004, http://wwwa101avn.org/genpetraeus.htm.

6. Cloud and Jaffe, *The Fourth Star*, 130.

7. Donna Miles, "101st Commander Calls Adaptability Key to Success in Iraq," *American Forces Press Service*, March 17, 2004, http://www.a101avn.org/genpetraeus.htm.

8. Smith, "Beyond Baghdad."

Chapter 14

TRAINING IRAQI
SECURITY FORCES

After a short stay back home in the United States in the spring of 2004, Petraeus was asked to return to Iraq, first to assess for senior U.S. leaders the performance of the Iraqi Security Forces (ISF) in the wake of the April uprisings, when only the ISF in Mosul did well; and then as the commander of a new Coalition organization whose mission was to organize, train, and equip the ISF. Leading the Multi-National Security Transition Team-Iraq (MNSTC-I) was not what Petraeus expected, but he was one of few senior leaders in the army with both the intellectual preparation and experience to take on this complex task. It would not be easy. While he was keeping Mosul and northern Iraq under control as best he could, events in northern Iraq in late 2003 and early 2004 began to turn swiftly against the Americans.

The army, and the army's chain of command in the Pentagon, had always planned to begin withdrawing forces after the fall of Baghdad and elimination of Saddam Hussein's regime. There had been some planning for the phase of operations that was to follow combat operations, but there was little heart in the effort, and the resources dedicated to it were inadequate. It was thus with as much hope as detailed preparation that the majority of the 130,000 troops in Iraq expected to be returning home soon.

The reality, however, was much different. Violence was erupting by the spring of 2004, and in whack-a-mole fashion, U.S. leaders were frantically, but mostly ineffectively, reacting to quell it. Like a wildfire, the fighting across Iraq—north, central, and south—began to combust in many places, seemingly at once. It appeared to the Americans that the rules had changed without their knowing and that now they were waging multiple wars simultaneously, none of which they wanted. In the north, Petraeus had managed to generally keep a lid on the smoldering embers, at least in the short term. His aggressive military operations coupled with equally aggressive, even ambitious, re-development of economic and political institutions kept the violent outbreaks manageable, at least until the 101st division was withdrawn, when it began to seem that perhaps his efforts in northern Iraq may have simply treated symptoms rather than causes.

Elsewhere, the signs of broadening troubles were undeniable. Violence in central and southern Iraq was spiraling out of control rapidly. Baghdad was a mixed bag; some U.S. units had met with success pacifying the neighborhoods in their areas of responsibility, but the overall situation was rapidly deteriorating. North and west of Baghdad—in the Sunni triangle, featuring the restless cities of Fallujah, Ramadi, and Tikrit, and home to many Sunnis still loyal to the former Baathist regime—fighters were taking to the streets in larger numbers, battling U.S. troops. In the south, the United Kingdom seemed to pacify Basra; however, as was the case in Mosul, it soon became apparent that insurgent factions had not been extinguished but had in fact simply taken a breather to grow and become better organized.

The tactics employed by U.S. forces often were not helping. The vast majority of U.S. troops lived on heavily fortified operating bases, isolated from the Iraqi population. When they traveled, it was frequently in high-speed convoys, gunners perched atop their vehicles and not hesitant to fire their automatic weapons at threats both real and suspected. The conduct of the American troops was easily explained—they were beginning to be attacked regularly. But their methods did not endear them to civilian passersby, whose opinions mattered greatly when it came to rooting out insurgents. For the moment, it was apparent that the United

States lacked a comprehensive, unifying approach to counter the escalating violence, which it desperately needed.

The fragility of the situation for Western organizations of any kind in Iraq became starkly evident on August 19, 2003, when a cement truck carrying high explosives drove into the wall of the United Nations' headquarters in Baghdad, killing 22 staff members. The attack had far-reaching consequences, demonstrating that the war had taken a grim turn. The United Nations reduced its staff from about 800 to no more than a dozen or so, and nearly all other international organizations, both public and private, quickly fled Iraq also. In a short time, the situation was left to the military forces of the United States, a sizeable contingent of about 10,000 UK troops, a smattering of Coalition forces, and of course, the Iraqis themselves to resolve.

As the United States faced these deteriorating conditions, it also found itself with the need to rotate back home the large military units that arrived in early 2003 to conduct the invasion. Unfortunately, U.S. plans had called for a rapid de-escalation of America's commitment, and replacement troops were not readily available. Hence, in some cases, the follow-on formations were much smaller than the original units, as had been the case in northern Iraq when Petraeus and his 101st division redeployed to Fort Campbell. Occupying the same territory as had Petraeus's soldiers was a task force of less than half the 101st's size. This was reason alone for increasing violence—fewer troops meant that less reconstruction, and less security, was being provided. U.S. leaders tried to keep to their conviction that they were still on course. In February 2004, there were fewer than two dozen U.S. combat deaths, the lowest since the invasion. And U.S. troop strength was down to about 110,000 (it would ultimately climb to about 160,000 two years later).

But as warmer temperatures heralded the arrival of spring across the country, any pretense that Iraq would settle down and the United States could continue with its intentions to depart went up in the smoke, and the fire of combat increased in cities that heretofore were unknown to most Americans. Places like Fallujah and Ramadi became symbols of the grit of U.S. fighting forces while also representing a mission suddenly gone awry. In March, the 82d Airborne Division departed, turning Fallujah, a city of some half million residents located 40 miles west of Baghdad, to Marine Corps units. The marines had been highly critical of army practices, in effect, privately blaming the army's methods for accelerating the growing insurgency. To signal to the Iraqis that marines were adopting a different approach, they arrived believing that a less confrontational approach would achieve greater success. Whether they would have been successful cannot be known, as days after their arrival, a team of U.S. security contractors who were driving through the city were seized and beaten, and their bodies were burned and then hanged from a bridge over the Euphrates River while crowds were filmed cheering their deaths. International public opinion was outraged, and now the die was cast for the resumption of war. Days later, marine and army units launched a ground attack to retrieve control of the city.

The battle ebbed and flowed for about a month, until in early May the United States declared the city to be sufficiently pacified that a newly organized militia loyal to the government could maintain control. This faith in the ISF proved whimsical as the remaining guerrillas began immediately to reconstitute their losses. The insurgency spread to the city of Ramadi, capital of Al-Anbar Province, and resistance would go on with increasing intensity there too. And it wasn't only the Sunni insurgents west of Baghdad who were taking up arms; the south-central Shia strongholds of Najaf and Kut were also now erupting. Incidents of violence against U.S. forces nationwide began to spike: from fewer than 300 in late March to double that number by mid-April. They wouldn't average fewer than 500 again for another four years.

U.S. leaders took away several lessons from the outbreak: First, the enemy in Iraq was no longer Hussein's regime; it was a range of insurgents with both Sunni and Shia loyalties. And second, the United States must find a way to credibly train and organize large-scale ISF, both military and civilian police. Doing so was the mission Petraeus was ordered to solve. He faced daunting challenges.

To date, the United States had not systematically addressed the requirement to create credible security forces for the central government. Instead, efforts had been locally directed and wildly inconsistent. American commanders simply didn't have the resources, or the inclination, to devote themselves to training Iraqis. Keeping their own troops alive and performing their duties was a full time job, and besides, many leaders considered most young Iraqi men to be threats and did not relish the prospect of assembling them in large numbers in close proximity to U.S.

units. In any case, there simply were no systems in place to identify, recruit, organize, fund, and equip any Iraqis who did volunteer.

So far, fewer than 10 battalions (a battalion is approximately 750 soldiers) had been created. Petraeus was eventually directed to stand up 10 divisions, about 100,000 total troops, as well as police and border police, along with the infrastructure and institutions necessary to sustain them. Petraeus recognized right away that much more was involved than simply training the Iraqis in military tactics. An entire supporting infrastructure, at the cost of several billion dollars, must be established if the resulting force was to be credible and able to sustain itself. Separate schools for officers and enlisted troops were needed. In addition, uniforms; personal equipment; weapons; vehicles; spare parts; barracks; and money for salaries, food, and command-and-control architecture were needed urgently. And then all of these new soldiers must be brought to in-processing centers.

Trying to build the kind of professional military force that was envisioned, while at the same time fighting an aggressive and spreading insurgency, constituted a tremendous challenge. Sunnis had populated the higher ranks under Hussein, but now Shias were in charge. Could Sunnis and Shias now trust each other enough to collaborate so closely? How would each group treat the other while performing their duties? These were critical political and cultural issues whose answers weren't clear.

Further complicating prospects was the fact that the culture of the Iraqi military, corrupted for decades under Hussein, simply was not prepared for the sweeping transformation that the Americans were now demanding. Graft, for instance, was an entrenched and accepted practice. Because the Iraqi government lacked modern accounting systems, pay could not be dispensed centrally. Rather, commanders were given funds directly to operate and pay their subordinates. Since they were allotted money according to the number of soldiers on hand, personnel rosters were grossly inflated. And inevitably, the rank and file who were present received little money and hence demonstrated little loyalty to their leaders or to their organization. When they went home on leave, they often took with them whatever equipment, uniforms, and even weapons that they could to sell.

Likewise, all relationships ran nearly exclusively straight up and down the chain of command. Units did not trust one another and cooperated poorly or, more frequently, not at all. Hence, organizational support was minimal; units couldn't exchange vehicles to be repaired, for instance. Nor could they be expected to receive logistical support, even if doctrine and practices existed that mandated it.

The current pace for instituting change was moving far too slowly. Building the ISF on a scale of one battalion at a time would take a year to field a single division. In the meantime, recruits that did exist were under extraordinary stress. Many had been killed at their induction stations; others had been pulled from vehicles and executed. Morale was plummeting.

The media jumped on the precarious situation in Iraq, citing the failure so far to establish ISF to stem the rising tide of violence. In midsummer, *Newsweek* magazine ran a cover story featuring Petraeus outfitted in his combat gear on the cover with the headline, "Can This Man Save Iraq?" It wasn't necessarily the type of high-profile attention that would endear him to the army's chain of command in Iraq, now led by General George W. Casey Jr., who had replaced Lieutenant General Sanchez several weeks prior. Petraeus and Casey were each committed to succeeding, and both had devoted their professional lives to the army, but they were a contrast in styles. Casey was a senior officer who had already served as the vice chief of staff of the army. He was a traditional-school soldier, more conservative and conventional than was Petraeus. While Petraeus had cultivated high-impact relationships with the media and academic elites in Washington and at West Point, Casey kept a lower profile and relied upon friends and colleagues within the army. Petraeus's accomplishments in Mosul with the 101st, and the success he had achieved in telling that story in the national media, had caught the attention of decision makers in Washington who were eager for a successful formula in Iraq. Before returning to Iraq to lead MNSTC-I, Petraeus had met with President Bush, Secretary Rumsfeld, and Deputy Secretary of Defense Paul Wolfowitz, a privilege rarely accorded to a rising three-star general. He had even received a phone call from Britain's prime minister, Tony Blair.

When it came to Iraq, Petraeus saw a narrow window of opportunity that was for the moment swamping MNSTC-I's capabilities. His staff numbered too few, just a handful of general officers and fewer than 200 personnel (over time there would be 1,500). He had to compete with the demands caused by the deepening conflict for resources, which simply were not ample.

In early August, Casey published the first Campaign Plan of the war. This overarching plan, which laid out the key U.S. objectives and identified the ways that American and Coalition forces were to achieve them, was a formal attempt to reset the entire approach to the war. It called for U.S. combat troops to contain the violence in Iraq long enough for Petraeus to create enough ISF to do the job. It still featured an aggressive timeline though. Casey hoped that the United States could begin pulling back in 2005. Despite such an unrealistic goal, this approach, summarized by pundits as "drawing down while ISF stood up," did acknowledge that the United States was responsible for what was happening inside of Iraq and could not withdraw as long as an insurgency was underway. It also meant that the initial intent to build an Iraqi military that looked like the American model, focused on mechanized warfare and designed to battle regional opponents like Iran, was completely unrealistic. What Iraq needed from its security forces most immediately was internal security, policing, and stability. This meant an entirely different type of organizational structure, one in which artillery and armor would play little part initially, and patrolling, small unit tactics, intelligence, and law enforcement would be prominent.

As Petraeus told *Newsweek*, it would take time to create new security forces: "You don't just flip a light switch. You don't build an army or police in a matter of months. This is a perilous mission." When discussing the new emphasis on leader training and fresh equipment that was witnessing the fruits of more than $3 billion in spending in the form of 13,500 pistols, 850,000 rounds of ammunition, and 900 vehicles, Petraeus said, "It's really flowing in now."[1]

By late summer, the Iraqi forces Petraeus was training had their first test since the springtime battles with insurgents in and near Baghdad. In Najaf, about 100 miles south of the capital, a U.S. Marine patrol approached the hiding place of Moqtada al-Sadr, the Shiite radical whose militias had been generating widespread violence in Sadr City, Baghdad's largest slum. Sadr's militia reacted by attacking U.S. and government personnel and facilities throughout the city. Several U.S. Army battalions and three of the newly stood-up Iraqi battalions were ordered to retake the city along with marine units already there. The ensuing combat was intense but seemed to validate the direction Petraeus was taking. While U.S. forces on the ground and in the air had done the bulk of the fighting, the Iraqi forces at least had stood their ground and had not fled. As the battle was winding down, Casey met with his senior leaders in Baghdad to confirm that they would stick with their plan to reconstitute the ISF. It would cost tremendous resources, but the ISF would be the path home for the United States

In late September, Petraeus penned an editorial, "Battling for Iraq," in the *Washington Post* that summed up many of the challenges and the progress he thought MNSTC-I was making. In it, he again noted, "Helping organize, train and equip nearly a quarter-million of Iraq's security forces is a daunting task . . . Doing so in the middle of a tough insurgency increases the challenge enormously, making the mission akin to repairing an aircraft while in flight—and while being shot at."[2]

But he noted that "eighteen months after entering Iraq, I see tangible progress. Iraqi security elements are being rebuilt from the ground up." Then he went on to describe in detail why he felt reason for cautious optimism: approximately 164,000 Iraqi police and soldiers (of which about 100,000 were trained and equipped), and an additional 74,000 facility protection forces, were performing a wide variety of security missions, including the delivery of equipment. Petraeus noted the fact that "Iraqi security forces are in the fight—so much so that they are suffering substantial casualties as they take on more and more of the burdens to achieve security."[3] He recited updated figures to demonstrate the extensive scale of efforts to outfit the new forces: more than 39,000 weapons, 22 million rounds of ammunition, 42,000 sets of body armor, 4,400 vehicles, 16,000 radios, and more than 235,000 uniforms had been delivered since July 1st. Petraeus noted that 40 army battalions were conducting daily operations alongside Coalition forces, and training academies had been established to graduate about 5,000 new police officers each month. He closed on a cautious note, stating that, "There will be more tough times, frustration and disappointment along the way."

It was not too much of a surprise when only weeks after this article appeared, the guarded optimism of the late summer went up in the smoke of further fighting. Incidents in which the ISF largely failed to meet expectations mounted. In early October, an Iraqi army battalion was sent to Samarra, where ongoing U.S. operations were underway. But in the wake of a car bombing, the battalion commander and several key leaders quit, prompting the virtual dissolution of the unit as most of the soldiers refused to keep fighting. A few weeks later, Petraeus presided over the graduation of a basic training class, noting that the freshly minted troops looked sharp. A few hours later, reports reached Petraeus that several of the vehicles carrying the soldiers home for postgraduation leave had been stopped by insurgents at a fake checkpoint. The recruits had then been summarily executed. Other units saw their soldiers beheaded and bombed. Petraeus took each of these setbacks personally. He felt responsible. "They were our guys," he lamented.[4]

Even Mosul, the place in which Petraeus had invested so heavily, had begun to come apart. Attacks continued to increase, and the police force largely evaporated in the wake of a full-scale assault by insurgents against the police station. Fed by foreign fighters transiting into the region from beyond Iraq, Mosul would ultimately prove to be one of the last bastions of insurgent activity. In the face of such challenges, Petraeus was no less determined. However, little seemed to be working. His efforts didn't appear lasting, and time was running out. To change momentum, he proposed to employ cohesive teams from the active duty brigades to support and advise ISF in their areas, but instead, 11-man teams of individual augmentees were used. This too had little effect. The United States lost nearly 150 troops during the summer of 2004, more casualties than were lost during the invasion.

By November, the rising violence had returned to Fallujah, where Casey was about to order a fresh offensive to finally seize the city from the insurgents who had reestablished control there. ISF troops were to join the offensive and fight alongside the Americans. But as U.S. troops moved into position, hundreds of frightened ISF soldiers ran away, including officers and commanders. Many others arrived with their units without their basic equipment. Clearly, the ISF was still not ready to conduct a major operation. The battle cost the United States another 50-plus dead and more than 400 wounded. The fact that the insurgents lost well more than 1,000 fighters was little consolation as the combat seemed to gain little more than destroying the insurgent network in the city once more. The disappointment and frustration in the American chain of command was palpable. Despite the momentum that Petraeus had cited, long-term deficiencies in the U.S. approach to the war were still undermining the readiness of the ISF, and so reasons for the setbacks were many.

A prominent shortfall derived from the well-intentioned but the culturally tone-deaf education American trainers were providing to the Iraqi recruits. Instead of living and fighting alongside the Iraqis as U.S. Special Forces troops had long done when training indigenous forces, Petraeus's trainers were largely drill sergeants and conventional soldiers accustomed to training Americans in the United States. They knew little of Iraqi culture and expectations and lacked operational experience in the Middle East. To remedy this, Petraeus created an academy north of Baghdad to immerse U.S. trainers in the fundamentals of preparing Iraqis. This too was only a partial answer, but full solutions were in short supply, and Petraeus would not admit that he couldn't create success from hard work and sheer perseverance.

However, unease wasn't only mounting inside of Iraq. In Washington, there was consternation too. Soon after the new year, Secretary of Defense Rumsfeld dispatched a team of investigators to Iraq to look into the ISF training strategy. It was evident that even more resources were needed beyond those already committed, especially in terms of institutional architecture such as more schools and more robust logistical systems, even though some of Petraeus's requests for reinforcements had simply gone unanswered. What was less clear was the number of ISF battalions that Petraeus and Casey thought they needed to quell the insurgency and thereby release U.S. forces to redeploy home. There were also persistent problems with the elite commando battalions that the United States had supplied and was allowing to operate. Several of these units, largely commanded by Shia officers, had been accused of abusing prisoners, especially Sunnis.

Petraeus was aware of the commandos' behavior and was working to stem any mistreatment, but sectarian conduct was a feature of the broader war, whose intensity was only increasing. By the spring of 2005, it was clear that the first effort by Casey and Petraeus at a quick establishment of ISF to take on responsibility for protecting the Iraqi people and ending the insurgency had largely failed to redress the ISF's shortcomings. Much progress had been made, but lower-ranking U.S. military officers by this point were seething with criticisms of their own regarding the chain of command. They could see that the United States was not winning and that comprehensive remedies must be found.

MNSTC-I had grown along with the scope of the mission, but still Petraeus lacked sufficient tools, especially training cadre. With responsibility for about 100 Iraqi army battalions and more than 130,000 police, MNSTC-I's staff of 550 just wasn't enough. And there was little prospect of reinforcements because the pressure from Washington, through General Casey, was to hold the line on U.S. troop numbers. This late in the war, the United States was supposed to be drawing down, not adding, forces, even if the situation on the ground warranted it. Instead, U.S. forces found themselves in recurring pitched battles throughout 2005.

There were significant successes to be noted. Petraeus would contend that the foundation for training a competent ISF had at least been established: schools, administrative architecture, equipment, and MNSTC-I itself were all signs of growing institutional capacity. And in January 2005, parliamentary elections were held, followed by a constitutional referendum in October and the election of a National Assembly in December. But despite these political milestones, the insurgency fought on. The number of attacks continued to increase, reaching 1,800 a month in the autumn. In sum, there were more than 34,000 attacks recorded in 2005, an increase from about 26,500 in 2004. So gains were being made, but in the midst of a still-escalating war. Petraeus could boast of many achievements when in September he passed command of MNSTC-I to his successor, Lieutenant General Martin Dempsey. Under Petraeus, MNSTC-I had blazed a new trail, offering the United States a way to prevail in Iraq that consisted of much more than simply battling insurgents in the streets. Petraeus clearly saw the challenges of the war more broadly than involving combat alone. But a year and a half of hard work had not yet paid off in full. Petraeus had put pieces in place at MNSTC-I that would enable success in a year or two, but for now, ISF troops were not playing a decisive role to restore order to their country.

So Petraeus departed Iraq for a second time and returned home with the war grinding on, a resolution nowhere in sight. Petraeus was tired, but resolute. He would have little time to take stock because the army chief of staff, General Pete Schoomaker, had a new role for Petraeus. Far away from the front lines of Iraq, Petraeus was asked to engage in an insurgency of his own—to pull and prod the army, and the defense establishment, into the doctrinal world of counterinsurgency, or COIN.

NOTES

1. "Can This Man Save Iraq," *Newsweek*, June 27, 2004, http://www.prnewswire.com/news-releases/newsweek-cover-can-this-man-save-iraq-75166612.html.

2. General David Petraeus, "Battling for Iraq," *Washington Post*, September 26, 2004, B07.

3. Ibid.

4. Cloud and Jaffe, *The Fourth Star*, 176, 177.

Chapter 15

CHANGING ARMY DOCTRINE
FOR A NEW WAR IN IRAQ

The duty Petraeus was assigned as commanding general of the Combined Arms Center (CAC) back at Fort Leavenworth, Kansas, in the fall of 2005 was no less than to remedy the American armed forces' doctrinal shortfalls by specifically providing the Pentagon with a whole new way of understanding the improvised explosive devices (IED) and, in so doing, find America's path out of the war in Iraq. While leading CAC, Petraeus would overhaul much of the army's training, education, and leader development programs. What had the most profound and immediate impact was the solution he crafted with a hastily assembled team of thinkers. It proved to be the revival of a long-neglected aspect of army doctrine, known as COIN—counterinsurgency. COIN was both a description of an identifiable kind of wartime environment whose primary feature was conflict with irregular enemy combatants and a comprehensive method for U.S. forces to operate in those conditions. The very first step to a new philosophy of COIN was to understand IEDs as not merely a bombs but the end result of a complex human and technical chain of events.

More than any other weapon, the roadside bomb, or IED, changed the character of the war in Iraq. More than any other single factor, it was the IED that forced U.S. leaders to confront the fact that Coalition forces in Iraq were truly in extremis, without either the intellectual or tactical tools necessary to counter this lethal threat. IEDs rapidly undermined the U.S. war effort in several ways. The explosions killed and wounded U.S. troops for sure, but in a strategic sense, they revealed that the Coalition was losing its grip on the direction of the war. If IEDs were being emplaced with increasing frequency, then either the insurgents were successfully terrorizing Iraq's citizens who were not reporting the activity, or the citizenry was acquiescing to the insurgents' fight against the Coalition and the Iraqi government. In turn, U.S. soldiers and marines became more suspicious of everyday Iraqi people they met on the street, of the leadership of Iraq's security forces, and of Iraq's political class in general. Finally, the images of IED explosions playing on both regional and international television and on the Internet empowered and emboldened the insurgents, leading to even more IED operations.

The IED is not just a bomb or explosive device; rather, it is a weapon system that in principle functions much like conventional weapons. To build, place, and detonate each IED necessitates a network of people with specific skill sets, financing, logistical support, communications, and technical expertise. IEDs thus reflect complex organizational structures, and if the Coalition wanted to end the insurgency, destroying the IED networks would be a critical task.

The number of U.S. forces being killed by IEDs was very high, about one-third of those lost in the first year of the insurgency, as well as more than half of those wounded severely enough to be evacuated out of theater. Because the IEDs caused such large explosions, the number of severely wounded was also high. Iraq was littered with large ammo caches left over from the Saddam Hussein era that Coalition forces had been unable to remove. Insurgents plundered these sites and reburied or hid the pilfered munitions. Thus, they had in possession a tremendous quantity of very high-caliber mortar, artillery, and rocket rounds that when detonated caused extensive damage.

Insurgents initially hard-wired many of their IEDs and then waited in hiding nearby to detonate the bomb electrically. U.S. forces quickly learned to look for wires and then trace them to the insurgent at the other end, rendering this kind of IED less effective. Enemy techniques rapidly evolved, so that by 2004, they were turning to remote-controlled methods, detonating IEDs with cell phones, timers removed from household appliances, and car alarms. This eliminated the need for tell-tale wiring but still confronted insurgents with the challenge of hiding the IED itself. To solve this challenge, they began placing explosives inside the carcasses of putrefying animals and hidden in the ubiquitous piles of trash that littered Iraqi streets. Broken-down vehicles, construction or barrier material, and the rubble of buildings also afforded plentiful opportunities for hiding IEDs. Sometimes, entire houses would be rigged as a sort of super-IED. Insurgents would shoot at or otherwise lure Coalition troops to a house and then flee the scene, triggering the IED in an attempt to kill large numbers of converging Coalition forces. Another method was to serially detonate IEDs, targeting medical teams, police, and firemen who responded to an initial explosion. Since U.S. forces were equipped primarily with soft-sided High-mobility multi-wheeled vehicles (HMMWVs) in the early years of the war, they remained vulnerable. Even when a variety of armor configurations were rapidly added to all HMMWVs that went out on patrols, the vehicle's original specifications as a utility vehicle simply never envisioned that it would be able to withstand powerful explosions. Hence, the HMMWV, while highly mobile and adaptable, would later in the war be replaced by mine resistant ambush protected vehicles (MRAPs), large vehicles with V-shaped hulls specifically designed to withstand and deflect IEDs.

An insurgent group typically contained several IED *cells*, or small, semi-independent groups of fighters who were assigned the task of employing IEDs. Each cell consisted of between 5 and 10 people. The cell leader communicated with the larger insurgent group and led the cell's planning. He worked closely with the financier, whose job it was to tap into the group's money networks to pay the cell members and to obtain necessary supplies. This could involve extorting neighborhood shopkeepers and residents or could even involve larger kidnapping schemes or the sale of contraband. An explosives expert with sufficient technical expertise to safely construct the IED was, of course, essential. Such talent was highly valued and not always widely available to insurgent groups. Coalition forces would often uncover the remains of IED cell workshops that featured insurgent remains or other evidence of premature explosions. Other cell members were involved in the actual execution of the IED—an emplacer to set up and conceal the IED at the target, a triggerman to oversee the detonation sequence, and a video cameraman to record the event to be used in recruiting and propaganda materials. Other insurgents could join the cell also, to provide extra security or transportation or to serve as lookouts.

When the United States invaded Iraq in 2003, it was ill-equipped to understand and counter IEDs. The army's overarching war-fighting doctrine remained AirLand Battle, the same set of ideas that Petraeus had learned at Fort Stewart decades previously. At the political and strategic level, the underlying premises of AirLand Battle, although developed independently, had become known as the Powell doctrine, named after the chairman of the Joint Chiefs and later secretary of state Colin Powell, who had himself built upon the tenets first formulated by the former secretary of defense Casper Weinberger. The Weinberger/Powell doctrine maintained that the nation should only go to war when matters of national interest were at stake, and only then with the endorsement of the American public. It fit well with AirLand Battle doctrine, because it logically followed that U.S. forces should employ overwhelming firepower to achieve their goals. This model fit well when wars were formally declared or waged primarily by conventional forces, as had been the case in the two world wars, Korea, and the Persian Gulf. However, its applicability regarding irregular war, or insurgency, was less certain. This had been a deficiency in U.S. military thinking for many years, even before the Vietnam War soured U.S. thinkers toward counterinsurgency efforts.

Combat with insurgents or guerrillas in irregular war has been a recurring feature of American military history. From the Continental partisans who operated in the Carolinas against invading British troops; to the extensive use of light cavalry, especially by the Confederacy, to conduct raids on Union logistical targets; to the lengthy campaign by the U.S. Army against the Indians in the decades after the Civil War, irregular war was well known by U.S. military leaders of the 18th and 19th centuries. But during this lengthy period, irregular campaigns were not undertaken purposefully. Rather, they were by-products or diversions. Irregular combat was governed by scant doctrinal or even regulatory prescriptions and with little coordination attempted to align with broader campaign or national strategy. In other words, irregular war happened alongside the margins of major military activity and, even when decisive, did not influence the organization and thinking of major conventional forces, whose performance, it was always assumed, would ultimately determine the outcome of all important conflicts.

This began to change when the Spanish-American War in 1898 first required the United States to organize and deploy a significant expeditionary force, occupy Cuba, and then fight a long counterinsurgency campaign to subdue a rebel army in the Philippines. World War I again obscured the need for counterinsurgency expertise, but recurrent expeditions to Central American states by the marines revived its importance until World War II, followed by the war in Korea, dominated the nation's attention. Only in the 1960s, as the U.S. fought a long and fitful counterinsurgency campaign, did COIN again become a serious topic. But the very difficulty of the war in Vietnam, coupled with the need to rebuild the army as a volunteer force and to regain the strength to counter the Soviet Union, meant that the army returned to a focus on conventional warfare. It was in this context that Petraeus first encountered AirLand Battle in the late 1970s and early 1980s.

Now, as Petraeus considered the development of a COIN doctrine, he knew that he faced a longtime challenge that had never been resolved by military planners. And in recent decades, the vast majority of army and marine leaders had never questioned the suitability of AirLand Battle; only a few had studied COIN seriously, and almost no one had any practical experience.

Assignment to command of the CAC at Fort Leavenworth was seen by some observers as a sideways step for Petraeus after a rough tour at Multi-National Security Transition Team-Iraq (MNSTC-I), but it was better understood as a smart move by Army Chief of Staff Pete Schoomaker to place Petraeus at a place in which he could exert lasting influence on army doctrine. CAC was the organization within the army's Training and Doctrine Command most responsible for operations and tactics education and for applying lessons learned to army doctrine. It was an ideal spot for Petraeus to launch into a complete revision in how the United States would fight a counterinsurgency campaign.

Petraeus approached the creation of the new doctrine in a typically unorthodox manner. In February 2006 he assembled a team of experts with wide-ranging expertise. Over the winter months, Petraeus had overseen the writing of a first draft, and now he wanted to hash it out with his team in person. The cast was decidedly unmilitary, because in addition to soldiers and marines, professors, writers, intelligence officers, and even representatives from nongovernmental organizations were asked to contribute. It was an astute way not only to test the manual's precepts as they emerged, but to build consensus for the final publication. Team building to include those who may otherwise be opposed was a technique that Petraeus would often employ, and it worked well on this occasion.

Over the course of two days of vigorous and detailed discussion, more than 100 contributors hashed out all aspects of COIN. Petraeus emphasized that he didn't want to produce doctrine for those using it in the field that mandated what to do, but rather that helped them learn how to think. After the conference, Petraeus put his writers at CAC back to work, extensively revising the draft. He personally edited the language, pouring onto the page the knowledge about counterinsurgency he had gleaned from decades of professional study. Such direct involvement by the army's senior leadership had not occurred since the formalization of AirLand Battle in the revision of the *Operations* manual of the 1980s. In early summer, Petraeus circulated the text for armywide comment. Early reviews were positive, as the army was eager for any intellectual capital that would help them find a way out of Iraq. But there was no doubt that Petraeus was proposing a radical body of ideas, ones that called for a wholesale change in how the nation's land forces must think about counterinsurgency.

Formally published in December 2006, Field Manual 3-24, *Counterinsurgency*, advocated an approach to war that was very different than the familiar Powell doctrine and its guiding principle that overwhelming military force against an identifiable enemy was the necessary prerequisite for war. As the new manual stated early in the text: "Counterinsurgency operations generally have been neglected in broader American military doctrine and national security policies since the end of the Vietnam War over 30 years ago. This manual is designed to reverse that trend."[1]

To replace the military's conventional thinking, Petraeus was promoting in FM 3-24 ideas that up to now had been best articulated (but largely ignored in the United States) by David Galula, a French miltary officer who participated in France's campaign to pacify Algeria. Galula, writing with forthright clarity in the early 1960s, outlined the fundamental point that in counterinsurgency, the *minimum* degree of power was the key to success. He noted the salient point now also being put forward by Petraeus and his team that "the population therefore, becomes the objective for the counterinsurgent as . . . for his enemy."[2] Hence, the key to the entire equation for COIN doctrine becomes the comprehension that the population's security becomes the central issue of any counterinsurgency campaign.

To achieve the population's security, Petraeus proposed in the FM a novel set of solutions involving not only combat operations, but the development of host-nation security forces, the provision of essential services by the host nation's government, the building of host-nation political legitimacy, and the restoration of civilian economic activities.

Echoing Galula, the FM opened by noting, "Political power is the central issue in insurgencies and counterinsurgencies; each side aims

General Petraeus sits with Iraqi children during a youth soccer tournament in central Baghdad, Iraq, March 1, 2008. One of the central tenets of the counterinsurgency doctrine that Petraeus developed and then implemented was to ensure that security was provided to the local populace so that a sense of normality could return. AP photo/Dusan Vranic.

to get the people to accept its governance or authority as legitimate." Further, "Insurgents use all available tools—political (including diplomatic), informational (including appeals to religious, ethnic, or ideological beliefs), military, and economic—to overthrow the existing authority." To prevail against them, "counterinsurgents, in turn, use all instruments of national power to sustain the established or emerging government and reduce the likelihood of another crisis emerging." Thus, "Long-term success in COIN depends on the people taking charge of their own affairs and consenting to the government's rule."[3]

The FM went on to note that while "insurgency and its tactics are as old as warfare itself," it was also true that "all insurgencies are different," and "insurgencies follow a similar course of development." In a comment no doubt defending the American—and Petraeus'—experience in Iraq so far, the FM asserted that "one common feature of insurgencies is that the government that is being targeted generally takes awhile to recognize that an insurgency is occurring. Insurgents take advantage of that time to build strength and gather support. Thus, counterinsurgents often have to 'come from behind' when fighting an insurgency." Therefore, if accurate, the United States and its allies yet had time to prevail. And in further defense of the course of the war so far, the FM stated that another common feature of insurgent conflicts is that "forces conducting COIN operations usually begin poorly." Thus important to the U.S. effort going forward was the maxim that "in COIN, the side that learns faster and adapts more rapidly—the better learning organization—usually wins."[4] In sum, *Counterinsurgency* laid out a blueprint that was still a feasible one for the United States to pursue. It demanded a complete revamping of the American military's approach to warfare if the United States wanted to win in Iraq and in other irregular conflicts, which would not be easy for a force that prided itself on mastery of the conventional battlefield. But it also held out the promise of success, and success was in great demand.

Soon after FM 3-24's publication, Petraeus received a call from Secretary of Defense Gates. Would Petraeus accept command of U.S. forces in Iraq? The opportunity it presented was not entirely unexpected, but it was by no means inevitable either. There were other more senior generals who were candidates also, and Petraeus had already spent several years in Iraq; perhaps he should wait for a different assignment. Washington's uniformed and political leaders were continuing to insist that the Coalition was making progress in Iraq, but to the troops on the ground, gains were difficult to see. What was unspoken was also well understood by all—the United States had one more chance to get things right in Iraq. America would succeed or fail in 2007 and 2008. The next commander there would bear that burden, or that chance. Either way, he would be making history.

In many respects, the promotion to the rank of full general that would accompany the assignment marked a fulfillment of his decades-long study of warfare. His ambition and accomplishments were being rewarded with the attainment of the highest uniformed rank available, and nobody could be said to be better qualified. Of course, the cost to his family, as was the case with so many soldiers, would continue to be steep. His son Stephen had attended several different high schools but still managed to graduate at the top of his class. Daughter Anne has prospered too, but Petraeus missed many of her important events also. Petraeus no doubt knew that the personal costs aside, he found profound satisfaction being at the head of military organizations, and he simply could not turn away from a return to Iraq.

During his congressional confirmation hearings in late January, Petraeus emphasized that the war in Iraq required foremost a political solution to be undertaken by the Iraqis. U.S. military forces were necessary to help make that happen, but military force alone would not be enough to bring the war to a conclusion. He was candid when stating there would be plenty of hard days ahead. Discussions about the war in Washington had become politically charged and volatile, but Petraeus assured that in all cases he would provide his best, objective advice and that if he thought that the United States could not succeed, he would say so. But "hard is not hopeless" he reminded his questioners.[5] Some senators proposed that reforms were needed to motivate the Iraqis. Instead of offering a carrot to the Iraqi government in the form of sustained U.S. military support, a stick in the shape of reductions of U.S. military forces should be threatened. Petraeus agreed that the United States needed to maintain leverage with its Iraqi partners but knew that rendering them vulnerable to the insurgency could only be harmful. He explained again that the premise of the new COIN doctrine was that first the population must be protected; then the necessary political accommodations could be instituted. Left on the table was a potential problem—what if the Iraqi government ultimately adopted goals or programs that were inconsistent with those of the Coalition? It was a challenge that Petraeus would have to work on very carefully, along with the diplomats of the State Department, but one that could not be answered for the moment.

Before departing for Iraq, Petraeus was summoned to the White House for a conference with President Bush. It wasn't their first visit together, and they maintained a cordial relationship. The president needed a winning general, and Petraeus wanted to be the leader that turned the war around. Petraeus may not have considered the moment, but his situation was much like the one that his hero, General Grant, had encountered in 1864, when he too traveled to Washington to take direct control of the nation's war effort. There were other historical parallels also, in which a new leader had taken charge and placed his forthright personality to direct a clear change in the direction of U.S. military fortunes. General Pershing in World War I, General Ridgway in Korea, and General Abrams in Vietnam were examples from the previous century. Now Petraeus was stepping up to be the first of the new century. Despite his talents and energy, however, the outcome remained much in doubt.

In the second week of February 2007, Petraeus took command of Multi-National Forces Iraq (MNF-I). He was promoted at the same time, pinning on his fourth star at MNF-I's headquarters, housed in another of Saddam Hussein's grandiose palaces. This one, named Al Faw, sat on a small man-made island in the middle of a man-made lake, teeming with large fish that soldiers darkly joked had grown fat feeding on the corpses of dead Iraqi generals that surely lurked on the lake bottom. The area surrounding the palace had been a former country retreat about a dozen miles west of the capital, a refuge and playground of water and villas for Baathist dignitaries who wanted to escape Baghdad's hot concrete and seething population. Reflecting the grim conditions in Iraq, the ceremony was done with little celebration and much determination. The violence in Iraq was continuing to escalate; in some months, as many as 3,000 lives, the vast majority Iraqi citizens, were being lost. Several hundred soldiers, along with a smattering of Iraqi officers and officials, assembled to hear brief comments by Generals Casey and Petraeus.

Casey appeared solemn and conflicted. He was proud, a man who had spent his entire life in the embrace of the army and who had seen his father, a general, killed in Vietnam, the highest-ranking soldier to die in that conflict. Casey no doubt believed that he had been dealt a difficult hand but that he had made gains by reorienting the U.S. war effort while doing all he could to preserve and protect the U.S. forces serving in the bewilderingly complex battlefield that Iraq had become. When it came time to speak, he struck an upbeat and complimentary tone, extending his regards to the listening Iraqis and to the broader audience of the U.S. public and political class in Washington. He was headed to the Pentagon to become the army's chief of staff, the service's most senior officer, responsible for training and organizing the entire force. His advancement served as clear recognition that he had given all he could to the army he loved as it fought and bled in Iraq. But the fact that he was being moved was also recognition that a new direction, and a new leader, was needed.

In honor of Petraeus, a military band played the 101st Division's song. Everyone there—and those not there—fully understood that this moment marked more than just the changing of the guard. Petraeus was not just the next commander. Rather, he would be a *new* commander, the man who would refashion the way that senior uniformed officers would relate to their political bosses and who would upend the entire U.S. military strategy in Iraq. In so doing, he would begin to drive the implementation of cultural changes in the army, and even the Marine Corps, that would entail organizational, doctrinal, and training changes to an extent not seen since the army returned from Vietnam. Petraeus was engaging, animated, and taut like a coiled spring. He always radiated energy, and it was no different this day. "The mission is doable," he noted.[6] It was clear that he believed it. It was equally clear that nearly everyone else had doubts. In his introductory letter to the troops, he emphasized what would become a hallmark of the COIN operations he led—ensuring security of the population.

Casey had started to turn the war in a new direction, but it was Petraeus who had been called to build upon the groundwork that others had laid. The talents and sweat, and even blood, of many, both named and unnamed, would contribute to the war effort going forward. But none of that would change the fact that from this day, Petraeus would bear the brunt of the criticism, or the credit, for America's enterprise in Iraq. The war was now his to win or lose.

NOTES

1. Department of the Army, *Field Manual 3-24: Counterinsurgency* (Washington, DC: Department of the Army, 2006), vii.

2. David Galula, *Counterinsurgency Warfare, Theory and Practice* (1964; repr., Westport, CT: Praeger Security International, 2006), 52

3. Department of the Army, *Field Manual 3-24*, 1-1.

4. Department of the Army, *Field Manual 3-24*, ix.

5. Robinson, *Tell Me How This Ends*, 81.

6. Cloud and Jaffe, *The Fourth Star*, 255.

Chapter 16

MNF-I: STARTING THE SURGE

The path that led to Petraeus's command of Multi-National Forces Iraq (MNF-I) had not been a direct one. While he had been busy crafting a new COIN, or counterinsurgency, doctrine from Fort Leavenworth, the war in Iraq continued to deteriorate. UN estimates put the number of Iraqi dead, nearly all killed by other Iraqis, at more than 30,000. The term *insurgency* was now accompanied in the media and halls of the Pentagon and Capitol Hill with the words *civil war*. Most U.S. leaders publicly refuted the term because doing so would be an admission of failure, but arguing that Iraq was not slipping into full-scale civil war became increasingly difficult to refute. Every morning, dead bodies were being found in the streets by the hundreds. Victims who had been bound and gunshot, many with wounds and burns that could only come from torture, were abundant. Baghdad and other major cities looked like battlefields, with blown-up vehicles, shattered buildings, debris, barriers, and barbed wire.

Admitting the downward drift of events in Iraq, in November 2005, the Bush administration published a broad outline for the war entitled the "National Strategy for Victory in Iraq." Recognizing that more than

U.S. military forces would be needed to address the fractures of postinvasion Iraq, the strategy outlined a solution that began to apply the broader resources of the U.S. government. Two bumper-sticker ideas stood out that had been seized by military planners in Iraq. The first was "clear, hold, and build" and the second was "as the Iraqi forces stand up, we will stand down."

By then, Casey was already operationalizing this strategy, but he was achieving inconsistent results. He sought to draw down the force from its size of 15 combat brigades to 10 in the fall of 2006, and then down to just 5 brigades by the end of 2007. But even months after Petraeus had departed Multi-National Security Transition Team-Iraq (MNSTC-I), there were still only about 4,000 U.S. advisors supporting about 300,000 Iraqi Security Forces (ISF), and the ISF still weren't able to take on sizeable independent operations. Any reduction in Coalition forces could only occur after the ISF were much more competent. Although Prime Minister Maliki's government had been inaugurated in May, and he promised that Iraqi army units would fully partner with U.S. forces to push back against the insurgency, casualties continued to mount with little sign of abating. In short, the plan simply wasn't working. Then, in November of 2006, U.S. domestic politics intervened to effectively put the Bush administration on the clock.

In midterm elections that month, Democrats seized control of Congress. Political observers on all sides agreed that the endgame in Iraq was now approaching, because the Democrats could now control funding for the war. They would have to be satisfied that the United States was on a clear path to success, or they would effectively demand a withdrawal. Pundits drawing parallels with the Vietnam experience now filled the media airwaves and public discourse.

Acutely aware of the pressure to produce results, a number of hurried studies were launched. National Security Advisor Stephen Hadley and Secretary of State Condoleezza Rice initiated a formal government review. Chairman of the Joint Chiefs General Peter Pace had started another within the Pentagon. But the report that first garnered the lion's share of attention was the publication of the findings of the Iraq Study Group (ISG), a high-profile bipartisan commission led by prominent dignitaries James Baker, former secretary of state; and Lee Hamilton, former chairman of the House Foreign Affairs Committee.

Not unexpectedly given the charged atmosphere in Washington and the nature of committee-style reviews, the findings were largely prosaic. Seeking to offend no one, the ISG advocated a series of half-measures that were politically sensitive to the American political situation, but not informed by a clear understanding of Iraqi politics nor the character of the insurgency on the ground. The ISG's report fundamentally resigned the Coalition to near-certain defeat in Iraq. Most of its recommendations were already underway, such as aggressively training ISF and engaging regional neighbors to assist with the situation on the ground. One controversial suggestion was that the United States should inform Prime Minister Maliki that the continued provision of U.S. support was to be contingent upon concrete demonstrations of progress. Unfortunately, this seemed to be a step as likely to produce resentment as progress. Overall, the ISG's report simply did not demonstrate a clear-eyed understanding of the underlying causes that were promoting instability and violence in Iraq. Thus, the ISG did little to resolve the debate over Iraq, and its report was promptly shunted aside by more-focused efforts.

The review that ultimately prompted the most significant change of course in U.S. policy toward Iraq since the 2003 invasion stemmed from debates that culminated within the Pentagon. Chairman Pace's team of officers had by December settled on several courses of action. One course was to commence a drawdown; another was to increase U.S. troop commitments; a third was to lower troop levels but sustain a longer-term training and advisory presence in Iraq; and a fourth was to increase troop numbers in the short term for a final push, then withdraw. Opinion regarding which option was preferable was split. General Pace leaned toward the final option, a surge of forces, but the army was reluctant. It was already strained from the frequent deployments and long war and knew that its readiness levels were slipping. It was becoming increasingly difficult to stay ready to deploy to another part of the world if the president called upon the army to fight elsewhere. Consensus was still absent. President Bush and his advisors wanted a path to success—and not immediate withdrawal—but a leading solution was still proving elusive.

In mid-December, the White House listened to a plan being advocated by retired general Jack Keane, a former vice chief of staff of the

army. Although no longer on active duty, he remained visible within
defense circles in Washington. Since the autumn he had been working behind the scenes to develop support for an evolving proposition
that the United States must fundamentally realign its war effort. He
concluded that the United States did need more forces but that any
reinforcements must accompany a change in strategy. The current
American plan to train the ISF was failing because the Iraqi government
could not organize new forces while it was still battling the insurgency.
The insurgency must be defeated first; then security forces would have
the space to mature, and at the same time, necessary political reform
would transpire.

Debates within the Pentagon and the White House persisted through
the holidays. Some argued for greater use of special operations forces,
others wanted conventional forces repositioned, and still others called
for the realignment of U.S. strategic goals. It wasn't clear to the public
which course President Bush would select. Then, amid U.S. deliberations over the course and cost of the war in Iraq, which had cost the
lives of about 30,000 Iraqis in 2006 alone, the world was treated to a
macabre reminder of the intensity of Iraq's sectarian passions.

On December 30, 2006, Saddam Hussein's execution by hanging was
surreptitiously video recorded by an Iraqi on his cell phone and posted
on the Internet. The video showed that Hussein had been taunted as
he was hung, giving the scene the look of mob vengeance rather than
the orderly enforcement of justice. Sunnis who saw the video no doubt
concluded that Prime Minister Maliki's Shiite-led administration could
not be trusted to treat them fairly. Instead of putting an end to a dictator's tyranny and signaling the beginning of a new era of responsible government, the execution simply fueled even greater animosities within
Iraq. And a sectarian vendetta played out in grainy footage on their
computer screens was certainly not what the American public expected
to see as the fruit of their country's occupation of Iraq.

The pressure for immediate change grew irresistible, and a change in
strategy from Washington was now inevitable. A new secretary of defense, Robert Gates, had taken office on December 18 and had flown
the next day to Baghdad after a quickly set-up meeting with Petraeus.
There Gates had assessed conditions firsthand. His predecessor, Secretary Rumsfeld, had become a lightning rod for opposition to the war,

General Petraeus earned the confidence of President Bush and senior administration officials by candid, detailed reporting from Iraq and by offering aggressive proposals to solve challenges. AP Photo/Steve Nesius.

and Gates now possessed a short window to effect a new direction. In meetings, General Casey remained steadfast that he was on track, but now Washington's—and the nation's—impatience swamped his best efforts. Nearly everyone agreed that from the beginning in Iraq, U.S. forces had been too few and that U.S. objectives had been too muddy. But the troops that were there simply hadn't been employed effectively, and hence success still seemed a long way off, if it could be retrieved at all. Too many soldiers and marines occupied bases that were too large, allowing the populace to be victimized in their neighborhoods every day and night by insurgents. And so far, the ISF had not, or could not, step up to quell the violence. The result was that sectarianism was running rampant and America was on the cusp of losing the war.

On January 10, 2007, President Bush declared a new plan for Iraq during a nationally televised address. After hearing Secretary Gates report from his travel, and after final rounds of deliberations with his advisors, he had concluded that the best course was to both reinforce U.S. troops in Iraq and adopt a new strategy. Days before, he had announced that a new leadership team would take charge of the war in Iraq.

In addition to his nomination of Petraeus to receive a fourth star, he also elevated Admiral William Fallon to lead U.S. Central Command (U.S. CENTCOM), replacing General John Abizaid. Fallon, as a navy officer, was an unusual choice to command the land-centric CENT-COM, which contained the countries of the Middle East. Fallon was known as a man who liked to closely supervise his subordinates, a trait that likely would not fit well with Petraeus's well-developed independent streak.

For now, however, the key element the president wanted to convey was not the personalities of his new commanders, but the fact that he was ordering more than 30,000 more troops to Iraq: five army combat brigades, several marine battalions, and appropriate supporting and enabling forces. He indicated that he had already digested the new doctrinal approach that Petraeus had publicized from Fort Leavenworth. The additional forces would be integrated within ISF units and would have well-defined missions. Their purpose was to secure Iraq's neighborhoods and to protect Iraq's citizens in their homes and shops. Sectarian vengeance would not be tolerated, and this included any by government troops. Other reforms would accompany the increase in forces. The number of reconstruction teams, small units of soldiers and economic experts that worked in the provinces to improve economic development and government services, would be doubled and would receive more funding for new projects. In all, it was a radically new plan for Iraq, the final and best chance the United States would have to finally turn the tide.

President Bush's affirmation of his commitment to the war in Iraq was greeted by fresh waves of violence as insurgents sought to communicate their own determination. On January 20, fighters of AAH (described below), a Shiite militia group allied with Iran, abducted five U.S. soldiers from a joint U.S.-Iraqi military post and then murdered them. The insurgents used a stolen SUV and wore American-style uniforms to gain entrance to the compound, an attack that demonstrated the growing sophistication and coordination of some militia groups. And this attack was not isolated; violence erupted across the country. Ten days later, a series of attacks by both Sunni and Shiite fighters against Shiite pilgrims, and a mortar strike in Baghdad resulted in more than 150 casualties. In Balad Ruz, about 50 miles northeast of Baghdad, a Sunni suicide bomber killed at least 19 and wounded 54; in Khanaqin, 100 miles east and north of the capital, a roadside bomb killed 11 and wounded 33; and back in Baghdad, two cars containing gunmen opened fire on a minibus, killing 7 and wounding 11. It was a bloody, but sadly characteristic, day in an Iraq that was spiraling out of control. And it was into this cauldron that Petraeus and the troops of the surge would be deployed.

The headquarters at Al Faw palace from which Petraeus would lead the Coalition war effort was located near the center of Camp Victory, a sprawling American installation adjacent to Baghdad International Airport. From Victory and its associated installations, Camps Stryker, Liberty and Cropper, the massive American war effort projected its influence to all corners of Iraq. At the time Petraeus took command, Coalition forces totaled about 130,000 overall. Usually left unsaid was that an equal number of contractors, many of them Iraqis, were also working for, or on behalf of, the Coalition.

Petraeus typically split his time between Camp Victory, Baghdad, and visiting units around the country. The bulk of the MNF-I staff worked out of Al Faw, and Petraeus lived with his personal team in a large, unremarkable house just across the lake from the palace, so the majority of staff meetings were held at Victory. Given their expanse and the presence of American-style amenities made available to the Coalition personnel there, daily life took on surreal form. Everywhere across the installation, alarms sounded frequently, indicating that a stray mortar or rocket round was inbound. Individuals scattered to seek shelter inside one of the ubiquitous concrete shelters placed just for that purpose, and then they returned to their business without comment. Explosions during the night usually merited little more than a glance out the window. It was just the norm for Iraq.

Petraeus traveled to the Green Zone in downtown Baghdad via helicopter most days each week, and depending on the what was happening, he sometimes spent portions of most days in the Green Zone, which was later renamed the International Zone, or IZ. Department of State diplomats were in the Green Zone, as were Iraqi ministries and portions of the MNF-I staff, particularly MNSTC-I, as well as large portions of the MNF-I operations staff. As had always been his habit, Petraeus slept little, working feverishly and long, sending e-mails and speaking on the phone far into the night. The seven- or eight-hour time difference between Baghdad and Washington meant that MNF-I staff fielded queries most heavily during the evening, as Americans were working through their day. What rest Petraeus and his senior commanders did get for themselves was often interrupted as military operations, especially assaults by special operations forces, occurred only when it was dark. These actions frequently involved situations requiring decisions by senior leaders.

Several days each week, Petraeus traveled around the country to visit units in the field. Staying visible was a central component of his leadership style. When he was inside of U.S. military compounds, he extolled the virtues of COIN doctrine and stiffened the resolve of his commanders, all the while listening carefully to the issues they raised. When visible to the Iraqi public, he was upbeat, shaking hands and slapping backs with shopkeepers and smiling warmly to kids. He strolled without helmet or body armor, giving the impression that he was just out for a walk with his friends. Privately, he was not afraid to rebuke Iraqi government officials and military officers when they fell short of his expectations.

Petraeus's energy provided a jolt to what had become a downtrodden military culture. He questioned everything and demanded rapid changes from his senior staff. He was stunned at the scenes of urban destruction he witnessed and often detoured his helicopter on *purple rain* flights to better survey cities from the air. What he saw—garbage, broken-down buildings, burning fires, wrecked cars—all pointed to a society on the brink of chaos. It was evident that he needed the surge brigades as soon as possible, but they were not yet ready. One was deploying quickly, but the others would not all be in place until June. It simply was going to take that long to train and equip them. Iraqi battalions were flowing to Baghdad, but they were not always manned properly. Coalition assessments called for more than 40,000 ISF troops to garrison the city, a number that could not be approached for many months. In the immediate term, Petraeus took the opportunity to plan how he wanted to assign the forces that were coming, a decision that he would take in concert with his chief subordinate, Multi-National Corps-Iraq (MNC-I) commander Lieutenant General Raymond Odierno.

General Petraeus and General Ray Odierno sit together in September 2008, during the MNF-I Change of Command ceremony. Petraeus and Odierno were the architects of the Coalition's success in Iraq. AP Photo/Paul J. Richards, pool.

MNC-I was the war-fighting command directly subordinate to Petraeus's MNF-I, and it was Odierno's duty to directly oversee the Coalition forces for operations on the battlefield. He had assumed command only two months previously, taking over from Lieutenant General Pete Chiarelli, who went on to become the army's vice chief of staff. Chiarelli had earned a reputation as an innovator who sought creative solutions involving on-the-spot political and economic solutions to mitigate violence on the ground. Odierno had begun the war leading the army's 4th Infantry Division. His unit had arrived after the initial invasion and had taken positions northwest of Baghdad in the dreaded Sunni Triangle. There they found themselves in the middle of the severe resistance from insurgents that erupted in 2004. Odierno fought back hard, and realizing that he was seeing only short-term benefits from the high-firepower approach, soon began transitioning to a more nuanced range of responses. Now, he would be the man that Petraeus would turn to on a daily basis to implement COIN doctrine. Odierno would be in charge of overseeing the movement of every major unit in Iraq. If Petraeus would prove to be the leader playing a modern-era Grant, then Odierno would initially play the role of General Sherman. And like Sherman, in time Odierno would prove not only to be an able lieutenant, but an astute observer of Iraqi politics and masterful commander in his own right.

The Baghdad Security Plan, also known as Operation Fardh al-Qanoon ("Enforcing the Law"), was launched on February 14, 2007. It had been first formulated by Multi-National Division, Baghdad (MND-B) planners in late 2006 as a means for pushing tactical responsibilities to the battalion level (battalions were 800-man units commanded by a lieutenant colonel and supervised by a colonel). The Americans created a number of districts across Baghdad and then assigned a U.S. battalion and Iraqi army brigade to each district. The districts were given names for the neighborhoods in their local area: west of the Tigris River were Kadhimiya, Mansour, Karkh, East Rashid, and West Rashid;, and to the east were Adhamiya, Sadr City, Rusafa New Baghdad, and Karrada. U.S. battalions would live alongside ISF units, conducting joint patrols and focusing on establishing security in the areas adjacent to their bases. Then they would begin patrolling farther through the city, protecting neighborhood after neighborhood. Once initial security was established, teams could focus on the initial steps necessary to restore economic activity and government services. The most critical part was the first step—establishing security. It was this piece that had been lacking so far in most U.S. and Coalition operations. Petraeus knew that if the population could be separated from the enemy militias, then citizens could begin the difficult process of reestablishing trust with U.S. forces and the legitimate Iraqi government. Of course, this presumed that the factions within the government would also improve their cooperation and would deliver the much-needed oversight and resources that Iraq's economy and local political councils so desperately needed. That too would require much of Petraeus's attention.

Petraeus would later describe this general strategy as the "Anaconda" approach. By that he meant a wide range of activities that when pursued simultaneously, would act to strangle insurgent groups by not only fighting them force-on-force, but equally importantly, denying them financing, recruits, supplies, communications, information, and intelligence. The entire network that supported and enabled insurgent organizations was now increasingly subject to disruption and destruction by U.S. forces.

As the surge evolved, Petraeus and Odierno constantly arbitrated the competing demands of the various subordinate commanders not just in Baghdad, but across Iraq, all of whom were clamoring for additional forces to secure their areas of operation. Baghdad was the barometer for all of Iraq—the fate of the capital would foremost determine the destiny of the rest of the country. Thus, in addition to securing it from within, the flow of insurgents into the city must be stemmed. The suburban areas surrounding the city had become way stations for insurgent groups, places of refuge and locations from which improvised explosive devices (IEDs) could be manufactured. These needed to be rooted out. In a similar fashion, Al Qaeda and other foreign fighters being recruited to battle inside of Iraq, along with their weapons and money, had to be stopped at the border. Up to 90 foreign fighters were crossing into Iraq from the west on a daily/weekly basis, and an untold number were being sponsored by Iran or even in their home countries, a problem that CENTCOM was taking on. While no single place was as critical as Baghdad, other areas were still important. The province of Diyala to the north and east was a scene of turmoil, as was the western province of Anbar. The city of Basra, in the far south, and Al Kut, Hillah, An Najaf, and Karbala, closer in, were also flash points. Ultimately, Petraeus and Odierno would decide to largely split the surge forces, assigning about half of them inside Baghdad, and half to the most urgent areas around the city.

One of the foremost challenges facing the Coalition, and one that made the situation in Iraq so difficult to comprehend was the multifaceted nature of the insurgency. Iraq was embroiled not in a single contest for power, but multiple violent conflicts that pitted ethnic, religious, and political groups against each other as well as the Coalition. Understanding how to address these threats was central to the application of the COIN tactics that Petraeus was championing now and would remain important to U.S. forces going forward. The enemy with a universalist focus was Al Qaeda, and its Iraqi component, Al Qaeda in

Iraq (AQI). Internally, Sunni and Shia groups fought each other for prominence.

The world's most notorious terrorist group, Al Qaeda, was established by Osama bin Laden in 1988. Formed around a cadre of Sunni Arabs who fought in Afghanistan against the former Soviet Union, Al Qaeda's declared goal has remained constant through the intervening years—the establishment of a pan-Islamic caliphate throughout the Muslim world and, ultimately, internationally. Toward this end, Al Qaeda seeks to unite Muslims to fight the West, especially the United States, which the group sees as the leading apostate nation. Al Qaeda revives the Salafist tradition within Islam, which elevates the early period of the faith and the pious elders, beginning with the Prophet Muhammad, as role models for contemporary believers. Thus, Al Qaeda's adherents abhor American society in every respect and see U.S. economic, cultural, and political influence as direct threats to traditional Islamic tribal life. Al Qaeda also blames the United States for the corruption of many Islamic regimes in the Middle East, attributing the existence of those regimes to American diplomacy. Al Qaeda issued a manifesto in February 1998 under the banner of the "World Islamic Front for Jihad Against the Jews and Crusaders" declaring it the duty of all Muslims to murder U.S. citizens and their allies everywhere they could be found and targeted. That a group could hold such hatred toward the United States was difficult for many Americans to understand and accept, and warnings concerning the havoc that such a group could inflict continued to go unheeded. Al Qaeda, however, demonstrated its seriousness by conducting bombings in August 1998 of the U.S. embassies in Kenya and Tanzania and orchestrating the October 2000 attack on the U.S. Navy ship USS *Cole* while it was anchored in the port of Aden, Yemen, killing 17 U.S. sailors and injuring dozens more. And then Al Qaeda took terrorism to new heights on September 11, 2001, when 19 Al Qaeda attackers hijacked and crashed four U.S. commercial airliners—two into the World Trade Center in New York City; one into the Pentagon near Washington, D.C.; and a fourth into a field in Shanksville, Pennsylvania. Nearly 3,000 innocent civilians died.

Since then, Al Qaeda and its allies have conducted attacks worldwide, including in Europe, North Africa, South Asia, Southeast Asia, and the Middle East. Sometimes Al Qaeda's ideology is enough to inspire attacks; the bombing of a Madrid commuter train was done by terrorists without any direct support from Al Qaeda itself. Al Qaeda has remained very active to keep its name in the news. In 2005, Bin Laden's deputy, al-Zawahiri, claimed Al Qaeda responsibility for bombings in the United Kingdom. In 2006, British security services foiled an Al Qaeda plot to detonate explosives on up to 10 transatlantic flights originating from London's Heathrow airport. Looking ahead, in 2009, extremist leaders in Yemen and Saudi Arabia announced they had merged to fight under the banner of Al Qaeda in the Arabian Peninsula. Of course, Al Qaeda remains present in the border area between Afghanistan and Pakistan, the area from which it originated more than two decades ago, and the place that its senior leaders are believed to be still in hiding.

Of the Sunni resistance groups operating in Iraq, AQI, also known as the Islamic State of Iraq, or Al Qaeda in the land of the Two Rivers, was the most prominent since its establishment in April 2004 by long-time Jordanian jihadist Abu Musab al-Zarqawi. By employing indiscriminate violence through means such as vehicle-borne improvised explosive devices (VBIEDs), suicide bombers, rocket-propelled grenade attacks, and videotaped executions including beheadings, AQI attempted to foster sectarian violence and to gain international media attention to pressure Coalition countries to depart Iraq. In October 2004, al-Zarqawi pledged allegiance to Osama bin Laden. The following year, as part of its plan to spread jihad into Syria, Lebanon, Israel, and Jordan, and to establish an Islamic state there, AQI expanded its targeting outside of Iraq. Within Iraq, AQI continued to foment civil war by targeting Iraqi civilians. They nearly achieved the civil war they sought when they bombed a revered Shia shrine in Samarra in February of 2006 and June of 2007, setting off a series of deadly reprisal killings between Sunnis and Shias. Over time, the emergence of anti-AQI groups, improved ISF operations, and successful Coalition targeting of AQI networks would gradually deny the terrorists their traditional safe havens and restricted their ability to plan and conduct attacks. However, the group remained active and dangerous, and large-scale, high-profile attacks against government ministries near the International Zone in Baghdad that caused hundreds of casualties in late 2009 were evidence of AQI's enduring lethality.

Al Qaeda was not the only Sunni terrorist group functioning in Iraq. Most Sunnis felt some degree of disenfranchisement and apprehension about the future now that Iraq's Shia majority was likely to retain control of Iraq's central government. Radical elements who organized themselves to commit violence did so in opposition to Shia authority foremost, and to U.S. and Coalition forces second because they saw Westerners as supporting Shia rule. Ansar al-Islam (AI), formerly known as Ansar al-Sunna (AS), was another Salafist Sunni extremist group composed of Iraqi Kurds and Arabs. Like Al Qaeda, it sought to establish an Islamic state under strictly interpreted Islamic law (sharia). AI operated primarily in northern Iraq and conducted attacks at a rate second only to AQI. The group was responsible for the bombing of a U.S. military dining facility in Mosul in December 2004 that killed 22 U.S. and Coalition soldiers. While killing ISF and Coalition troops was common, AI did not hesitant to wage violence against civilians and to assassinate third-party nationals they captured.

A similar terrorist organization was the 1920 Revolution Brigades, consisting largely of former members of the disbanded Iraqi army. The group's name refers to the 1920 revolution by Iraqis against British colonial rule, thus drawing a parallel between the resistance then and the guerrillas fighting Coalition forces today. A group that claimed affinity with a different branch of Islamic theology was the Men of the Army of al-Naqshbandia Way (Jaysh Rajal al-Tariqah al-Naqshbandia, or JRTN), a Sufi order of Sunni jihadists who announced insurgency operations against the Coalition in Iraq in December 2006 in response to the hanging of Saddam Hussein that month. While Sufism is traditionally viewed as a nonviolent, mystical form of Islam that professes to seek spiritual unity, this group harnessed their Islamic identity in the service of armed attacks. The Naqshbandi army claimed numerous attacks against the Coalition, posting links to video clips of these attacks in various online forums. Like some other insurgency groups, JRTN published a monthly magazine promoting the group's ideology and enumerating its operations against Coalition forces while soliciting donations.

The Shia militia threat consisted of a different constellation of groups, including Asa'ib Ahl al-Haq (AAH), the Promised Day Brigade (PDB),

Kataib Hezbollah (KH), and various splinter organizations. These Shia militants typically received some measure of financing, training, and support from Iran, and their general purpose was to expel the Coalition as a means to installing a Shia government in Baghdad that was friendly to Iranian aspirations to control Iraqi affairs. The Shia were determined not to allow the Sunni minority to take power as had happened in the early years of the 20th century when the British pulled out of Iraq in the wake of World War I. At that time, Sunni leaders grasped the reigns of power, leaving the Shia marginalized ever since.

AAH, a Shia militia whose leaders were formerly close associates of Moqtada al-Sadr, was originally formed as an elite faction of Sadr's broader movement, Jaysh al-Mahdi (JAM), in late 2004. Sadr was a fiery young cleric with a degree of street sense but lacking strong leadership qualities. JAM had been created by Sadr in July 2003 to oppose the Coalition in Iraq, staging major uprisings in the spring and summer of 2004. It was also heavily involved in the sectarian conflict that erupted after the February 2006 bombing of the al-Askari Shrine in Samarra. Coming under popular pressure as well as feeling the effects of both government and Coalition security forces, Sadr would order a freeze on all JAM activity in August 2007. The following summer, Sadr announced that JAM would be transitioned into a sociocultural organization to oppose secularism and Western thought while a small group of handpicked fighters would continue to target the Coalition. In mid-November 2008, Sadr declared the formation of the PDB, providing a name for the authorized militia. AAH members, however, argued that Sadr's reorganization was mistaken and that they were the faction that best upholds the teachings of al-Sadr's father, the late Grand Ayatollah Muhammad Sadiq al-Sadr. Their dispute has continued, and Sadr, who soon took up residence in Iran, began to witness diminishment of his stature as a result. AAH terrorists, given their Iranian links, were capable of executing very powerful IEDs, rocket-propelled mortars, and EFP attacks.

Kataib Hezbollah (KH) is not large in numbers and has not undertaken many attacks relative to other terrorist organizations, but given close ties to Iran, its violence has been exceptionally lethal. KH leverages a close relationship with Iran to acquire sophisticated weapons, such as improvised rocket assisted mortars (IRAMs), man-portable air-defense systems (MANPADS), IEDs, and EFPs. It typically does not target Iraqi civilians, saving the majority of its assaults for Coalition and government security forces. Aggressive U.S. targeting has severely constrained KH activities, but this group retains significant capability to inflict violence.

To combat this host of enemies, Petraeus understood better than any other senior leader in America's armed services that he needed to clearly articulate how the surge forces were to be assigned missions, how the Anaconda strategy was to be implemented, and how COIN doctrine was to take shape on the ground. As he later told an interviewer,

> In the position I occupied in Iraq as the commander of our forces there, what I could do and sought to do was establish the big ideas. An example is the counterinsurgency guidance. Those were the big ideas that guided us in Iraq. And you have to be able to communicate them effectively. . . . And you just echo it and re-echo it in every forum, in every communications opportunity you have.[1]

Thus, the relentless communicator Petraeus took pen in hand to broadcast to his commanders and troops how they were to accomplish Coalition objectives on the ground in Iraq. Petraeus built upon an article he had written in 2006 for the journal *Military Review* in which he listed 14 observations from his time in Iraq. Now he again drew up a how-to checklist for day-to-day tactical counterinsurgency operations that was intended to be understood and followed by every member of the command. In it, Petraeus emphasized in direct language how his subordinates were to approach the complex demands of irregular warfare facing them.

Adopting a straightforward tone, Petraeus listed succinct doctrinal precepts that he had first formalized in the army's new COIN doctrine that he had authored at Fort Leavenworth and subsequently fine-tuned as America's military commander in Iraq. Then, by illustrating each tenet in practical, and even colorful, terms, Petraeus created a primer that colonels and privates alike could grasp. The character of the guidance belied what was a comprehensive declaration of Petraeus's revolutionary command style. Rarely did a four-star general offer a blueprint for waging a military campaign in such clear and public terms, and even more rarely did one capture an entire way of waging war in a way that harnessed the energies and talents of so many rank and file toward shared objectives. It was a case of applied, intellectual leadership that was one of Petraeus's hallmarks, an instance of getting the big ideas on paper, understood, and then communicated throughout a large organization. Soon taped to the walls of unit dayrooms and mess halls (and later modeled by other senior commanders who would issue similar guidance documents tailored to their areas of responsibility), Petraeus's key points included the following:

- **Secure and serve the population.** The Iraqi people are the decisive "terrain." Together with our Iraqi partners, work to provide the people security, to give them respect, to gain their support, and to facilitate establishment of local governance, restoration of basic services, and revival of local economies.
- **Live among the people.** You can't commute to this fight. Position Joint Security Stations, Combat Outposts, and Patrol Bases in the neighborhoods we intend to secure. Living among the people is essential to securing them and defeating the insurgents.
- **Hold areas that have been secured.** Once we clear an area, we must retain it. Develop the plan for holding an area before starting to clear it. The people need to know that we and our Iraqi partners will not abandon them. When reducing forces, gradually thin our presence rather than handing off or withdrawing completely. Ensure situational awareness even after transfer of responsibility to Iraqi forces.
- **Pursue the enemy relentlessly.** Identify and pursue Al Qaeda-Iraq and other extremist elements tenaciously. Do not let them retain support areas or sanctuaries. Force the enemy to respond to us. Deny the enemy the ability to plan and conduct deliberate operations.
- **Employ all assets to isolate and defeat the terrorists and insurgents.** Counter-terrorist forces alone cannot defeat Al-Qaeda and the other extremists. Success requires a comprehensive approach that employs all forces and all means at our

disposal—non-kinetic as well as kinetic. Employ Coalition and Iraqi conventional and special operations forces, Sons of Iraq, and all other available non-military multipliers in accordance with the "Anaconda Strategy."

- **Generate unity of effort.** Coordinate operations and initiatives with our embassy and interagency partners, our Iraqi counterparts, local governmental leaders, and non-governmental organizations to ensure all are working to achieve a common purpose.

- **Promote reconciliation.** We cannot kill our way out of this endeavor. We and our Iraqi partners must identify and separate the "irreconcilables" from the "reconcilables" through thorough intelligence work, population control measures, information operations, kinetic operations, and political initiatives. We must strive to make the reconcilables part of the solution, even as we identify, pursue, and kill, capture, or drive out the irreconcilables.

- **Defeat the network, not just the attack.** Focus to the "left" of the explosion. Employ intelligence assets to identify the network behind an attack, and go after its leaders, explosives experts, financiers, suppliers, and operators.

- **Foster Iraqi legitimacy.** Encourage Iraqi leadership and initiative; recognize that their success is our success. Partner in all that we do and support local involvement in security, governance, economic revival, and provision of basic services. Find the right balance between Coalition Forces leading and the Iraqis exercising their leadership and initiative, and encourage the latter. Legitimacy of Iraqi actions in the eyes of the Iraqi people is essential to overall success.

- **Punch above your weight class.** Strive to be "bigger than you actually are." Partner in operations with Iraqi units and police, and employ "Sons of Iraq," contractors, and local Iraqis to perform routine tasks in and around Forward Operating Bases, Patrol Bases, and Joint Security Stations, thereby freeing up our troopers to focus on tasks "outside the wire."

- **Employ money as a weapon system.** Money can be "ammunition" as the security situation improves. Use a targeting board process to ensure the greatest effect for each "round" expended and to ensure that each engagement using money contributes to the achievement of the unit's overall objectives. Ensure contracting activities support the security effort, employing locals wherever possible. Employ a "matching fund" concept when feasible in order to ensure Iraqi involvement and commitment.

- **Fight for intelligence.** A nuanced understanding of the situation is everything. Analyze the intelligence that is gathered, share it, and fight for more. Every patrol should have tasks designed to augment understanding of the area of operations and the enemy. Operate on a "need to share" rather than a "need to know" basis. Disseminate intelligence as soon as possible to all who can benefit from it.
- **Walk.** Move mounted, work dismounted. Stop by, don't drive by. Patrol on foot and engage the population. Situational awareness can only be gained by interacting with the people face-to-face, not separated by ballistic glass.
- **Understand the neighborhood.** Map the human terrain and study it in detail. Understand the local culture and history. Learn about the tribes, formal and informal leaders, governmental structures, religious elements, and local security forces. Understand how local systems and structures—including governance, provision of basic services, maintenance of infrastructure, and economic elements—are supposed to function and how they really function.
- **Build relationships.** Relationships are a critical component of counterinsurgency operations. Together with our Iraqi counterparts, strive to establish productive links with local leaders, tribal sheikhs, governmental officials, religious leaders, and interagency partners.
- **Look for Sustainable Solutions.** Build mechanisms by which the Iraqi Security Forces, Iraqi community leaders, and local Iraqis under the control of governmental institutions can continue to secure local areas and sustain governance and economic gains in their communities as the Coalition Force presence is reduced. Figure out the Iraqi systems and help Iraqis make them work.

- **Maintain continuity and tempo through transitions.** Start to build the information you'll provide to your successors on the day you take over. Allow those who will follow you to "virtually look over your shoulder" while they're still at home station by giving them access to your daily updates and other items on SIPRNET [classified computer network]. Deploy planners and intel analysts ahead of time. Encourage extra time on the ground during transition periods, and strive to maintain operational tempo and local relationships to avoid giving the enemy respite.

- **Manage expectations.** Be cautious and measured in announcing progress. Note what has been accomplished, but also acknowledge what still needs to be done. Avoid premature declarations of success. Ensure our troopers and our partners are aware of our assessments and recognize that any counterinsurgency operation has innumerable challenges, that enemies get a vote, and that progress is likely to be slow.

- **Be first with the truth.** Get accurate information of significant activities to the chain of command, to Iraqi leaders, and to the press as soon as is possible. Beat the insurgents, extremists, and criminals to the headlines, and pre-empt rumors. Integrity is critical to this fight. Don't put lipstick on pigs. Acknowledge setbacks and failures, and then state what we've learned and how we'll respond. Hold the press (and ourselves) accountable for accuracy, characterization, and context. Avoid spin and let facts speak for themselves. Challenge enemy disinformation. Turn our enemies' bankrupt messages, extremist ideologies, oppressive practices, and indiscriminate violence against them.

- **Fight the information war relentlessly.** Realize that we are in a struggle for legitimacy that will be won or lost in the perception of the Iraqi people. Every action taken by the enemy and our forces has implications in the public arena. Develop and sustain a narrative that works and continually drive the themes home through all forms of media.

- **Live our values.** Do not hesitate to kill or capture the enemy, but stay true to the values we hold dear. Living our values distinguishes us from our enemies. There is no tougher endeavor than the one in which we are engaged. It is often brutal, physically demanding, and frustrating. All of us experience moments of anger, but we can neither give in to dark impulses nor tolerate unacceptable actions by others.

- **Exercise initiative.** In the absence of guidance or orders, determine what they should be and execute aggressively. Higher level leaders will provide a broad vision and paint "white lines on the road," but it will be up to those at tactical levels to turn "big ideas" into specific actions.
- **Empower subordinates.** Resource to enable decentralized action. Push assets and authorities down to those who most need them and can actually use them. Flatten reporting chains. Identify the level to which you would naturally plan and resource, and go one further—generally looking three levels down, vice the two levels down that is traditional in major combat operations.
- **Prepare for and exploit opportunities.** "Luck is what happens when preparation meets opportunity" (Seneca the Younger). Develop concepts (such as that of "reconcilables" and "irreconcilables") in anticipation of possible opportunities, and be prepared to take risk as necessary to take advantage of them.
- **Learn and adapt.** Continually assess the situation and adjust tactics, policies, and programs as required. Share good ideas. Avoid mental or physical complacency. Never forget that what works in an area today may not work there tomorrow, and that what works in one area may not work in another. Strive to ensure that our units are learning organizations. In counterinsurgency, the side that learns and adapts the fastest gains important advantages.[2]

This manifest amounted to Petraeus's big ideas about how to prosecute the war in Iraq. He would be given all of the available forces that could be sent to Iraq to implement them. Thus, he had both the ways and means at hand for another campaign. Now it was up to him and his chief commanders to find a way to success where so many other new starts had stalled.

NOTES

1. Brian O'Keefe, "General Petraeus on Leadership," *CNNMoney. com*, March 5, 2010, http://money.cnn.com/2010/03/04/news/compa nies/petraeus_leadership.fortune/index.htm.

2. General David Petraeus, "Multi-National Force-Iraq Commander's Counterinsurgency Guidance," July 2008. Headquarters MNF-I, Bagh-dad, Iraq.

Chapter 17

TURNING THE TIDE
IN IRAQ

Petraeus at least would have better tools with which to wage his campaign than had been available to his predecessors in Iraq, and more of them. At its height, force levels in Iraq, due in part to the surge, meant that about 170,000 troops were deployed to Multi-National Forces Iraq (MNF-I). And arriving army brigades were now being equipped with either Stryker combat vehicles or mine resistant ambush protected vehicles (MRAPs). MRAPs were designed specifically to replace high-mobility multi-wheeled vehicles (HMMWVs) and featured much greater carrying capacity and advanced armor protection. They are large wheeled vehicles, weighing about 20 tons, and come in a variety of configurations. Their chief feature is a V-shaped hull, designed specifically to counter the improvised explosive device (IED) threat by diverting blast effects up and away from the vehicle's occupants. Soldiers typically gave the MRAPs high praise, as MRAPs saved lives on many occasions. Strykers were adopted by the army in 2002 as a modern, medium-weight fighting platform suitable for the kind of urban conflict that Iraq became. The Strykers became the centerpiece of some army brigades, which were built around the advanced computer and information systems onboard the Strykers. Weighing about 18 tons, Strykers were also wheeled like the MRAPs but were designed from the ground up to be infantry carriers, command-and-control platforms, and fighting vehicles. While offering less protection against large roadside bombs than MRAPs, they were fully armored to defend against direct fire, could travel at a high speed, were highly maneuverable, and had high-tech electronics that provided soldiers with unparalleled situational awareness.

Nonetheless, Petraeus's early months in command of MNF-I were difficult. Maliki's administration had entered rough waters, and Petraeus, mindful that success in Iraq depended ultimately upon a political resolution of Iraq's difficulties, turned to the new U.S. ambassador in Iraq, Ryan Crocker, an expert in the region, who arrived to Baghdad in late March. Crocker was talented, credible, and kept a low profile—quite a contrast to Petraeus. But the two men got along very well, and they fashioned a close and effective relationship, meeting most days and talking daily. They ensured that their respective staffs assiduously coordinated activities to present to the Iraqi government a single U.S. position, not an easy task given the preconceptions that soldiers and diplomats often harbor about each other. Audiences with Maliki were nearly always jointly held, with both Crocker and Petraeus attending and speaking. Crocker was careful to appear levelheaded and deliberate, while Petraeus allowed more of his passion to show itself, whether it be genuine or manufactured for the Iraqis' benefit. In short, theirs was a model of military-civil cooperation.

Maliki had yet to garner the loyalty of many Sunnis, but for the moment, he was facing more urgent challenges from the Shia community, especially in Baghdad. Shia militias loyal to Moqtada al-Sadr were beginning to act more like a criminal mafia than a legitimate religious movement, and Sadr was encouraging their resistance. They were randomly seizing Sunnis and holding them for ransom or killing them, extorting shop owners and robbing from anyone they could. A number of Maliki's civil servants were increasingly loyal to Sadr's men and were accepting bribes or funneling government funds to them. The Ministry of Health was particularly corrupted. Crocker and Petraeus confronted Maliki with these facts, but it was a hard sell. U.S. special operations forces were obtaining abundant evidence that Sadr was receiving support from Iran to run his illegal rackets, and his militias were receiving training and munitions that they were using to attack Coalition troops. Maliki, who had lifelong ties to Iran, understood this but found it difficult to move too aggressively. He reassured the U.S. leaders that he would root out the crim-

U.S. ambassador to Iraq Ryan Crocker, right, speaks as General Petraeus, the top U.S. commander in Iraq, looks on during a press conference in September 2007. The close relationship forged by Crocker and Petraeus linked diplomatic and military efforts and proved critical to the Coalition's progress in Iraq. AP Photo/Akira Suemori.

inals, but Crocker and Petraeus knew it would be a deliberate process. They would have to maintain the pressure on the prime minister.

Expectations in Washington for immediate payoff from the surge were high—too high. A funding bill for the war passed Congress in May with the stipulation that the administration, which Petraeus knew to mean him personally, report in the autumn regarding the progress of the war. As Petraeus commented, Washington's clock was running faster than Baghdad's clock. Yet he knew that progress did need to be achieved to sustain America's political will. It meant that dramatic gains must be made that summer, or the war could effectively be lost, not due to the insurgents, but because Washington, along with the broader U.S. public, might lose the will to go any further. To forestall this, Petraeus aggressively leveraged his media networks and talents to invite think-tank experts, pundits, and journalists to Iraq, providing them access and telling the story of the U.S. effort. He was confident that if the story of how the United States was adapting in Iraq could be told, it would convince Americans to continue their support.

One way to change the calculus was through more aggressive reconciliation with individuals who had been opposing the government and the Coalition, but who could be turned around. Hence Petraeus pushed his staff at MNF-I to identify influential Iraqis whose loyalty could be developed through outreach to them. Criminals were avoided, but there were few angels on the battlefield of Iraq, so Petraeus's team worked with a variety of characters who were willing to change their resistance and who agreed to act constructively to build the new kind of society that was sought for in Iraq. Reconciliation was simply a way to build political capital, and it was a key component of the Joint Campaign Plan that MNF-I and the embassy jointly published in July. But reconciliation wouldn't be enough to win the war. Combat operations constituted the main line of operation for Petraeus's troops. In April and May, U.S. casualties had spiked, and more than any other statistic, that one had to be driven down.

Thus in June, with the five surge brigades and their enabling forces to provide surveillance and other supporting capacity in place, Petraeus launched a major offensive featuring high-intensity operations across the country. U.S. forces struck Al Qaeda hideouts and bomb-making factories around Baghdad and interdicted their traditional transportation routes from the north. Special operations troops conducted a series of raids that recovered numerous items of intelligence value. Things like correspondence, biometric evidence, financial records, and detainees led to even further raids. With Al Qaeda's networks under simultaneous assault and many of their leaders being taken off the battlefield, the terrorists lost tremendous capacity. Attacks against the Coalition peaked in June, remained high in early July, and then began declining precipitously through August, reaching levels not seen since 2005 by the end of the month. Security incidents would never again return to the elevated levels of spring and summer 2007.

On August 28, Jaysh al-Mahdi (JAM) militias, in what amounted to a bid for supremacy among Shia militia factions, attacked the Imam Hussein shrine in the city of Karbala, one of the holiest sites of Shia Islam. The Iraqi Security Forces (ISF) had expected that Sunni fighters might conduct an attack, but violence by Shia militants initially caught them by surprise. JAM militia opened fire with automatic weapon during a religious holiday when the streets were crowded with tens of thousands of pilgrims. The ensuing battle resulted in more than 100 casualties and prompted a harsh response from Maliki, who ordered a full clampdown by the ISF. House-by-house searches for the perpetrators ensued, and the pressure on Sadr himself grew so intense that he ordered JAM to adhere to a cease-fire. It was a significant victory for Maliki and the ISF, who proved that they would place Iraq above their own sectarian identity as Shias and stand up to criminal behavior wherever it was found. It was by no means the end of sectarian bias in the government, but it was a step in the right direction.

Petraeus took it as a signal that the political foundations of good governance that he and Crocker had been working for so assiduously were taking root. And the performance of the ISF in the Karbala fighting demonstrated their growing capabilities too. This event, coupled with the major successes against Al Qaeda around Baghdad and in the northern provinces, provided solid evidence that Petraeus's campaign was working. The atmosphere of the U.S. forces inside of Iraq was to keep pressing forward. But whether the Pentagon would stay committed to the high force levels in Iraq was, however, a question that had not been fully concluded. So when he returned to the United States to update his chain of command, Petraeus first had to argue that the surge should not be curtailed.

As the Karbala attack was winding down, Petraeus updated Admiral Fallon, Chairman Pace, and the service chiefs of staff. Most wanted brigades in Iraq to return as soon as possible. They argued that other competing strategic interests were at risk because the services, especially the army and the Marine Corps, did not have sufficient numbers of troops available to react to any contingency that might arise. The question came down to balancing risk—how much risk should the United States take in Iraq, and how much in other areas of the world? After updating Secretary Gates, Petraeus briefed President Bush. The president listened carefully to Petraeus and considered the competing points of view. The meeting ended with the president agreeing with Petraeus. He would fight the war already underway and take risk that another could erupt elsewhere.

Petraeus, along with Ambassador Crocker, next faced the prospect of updating Congress and, by doing so, informing the American public.

Emotions were raw over the subject of Iraq, and public figures and organizations staked out their positions in terms that were sometimes caustic. The most prominent was the biting personal attack by the progressive group Moveon.org, which took out an ad in the *New York Times* with a headline that blared, "General Petraeus or General Betray Us?" Petraeus took the ad hominem assault in stride, sticking to a factual recounting of events in Iraq. In carefully worded terms, he argued the case that the surge was working and that genuine progress was occurring in Iraq. He presented charts and cited the facts that violence had declined measurably, as had the number of civilian deaths in recent months. In a veiled reference to the debates that he had just concluded in the Pentagon, he noted that about 1,000 attacks were still occurring each week, a number still much higher than the 600 weekly attacks in 2004. So there was still a need for the forces in Iraq to stay in place. He attributed the success underway to a number of things: conventional and unconventional military strikes against insurgent cells; the protection of the populace being accomplished by troops living in local neighborhoods; the improved performance of the ISF; the effects of reconciliation outreach efforts, which were removing some militant leaders from opposition to the government; political reforms that were beginning to clean up the national ministries; and the positive influence of development activities. Petraeus went on to recommend that the ISF, especially the national police, continue to be trained and equipped, rather than disbanded as some observers were recommending. He finished by stating that the surge forces should remain in place, to be withdrawn sequentially later, but not right then. His goal was to go from the current equivalent of 20 brigades, to 15 brigades by mid-2008. During the next half day, legislators used the national stage afforded by the hearings to articulate their own views, a few supportive of Petraeus and Crocker, many adversarial. At the end of the noisy and intense hearing and the media whirlwind of the subsequent days, Petraeus had preserved sufficient political capital to continue his campaign. It had been a contest every bit as important as a military operation in the streets of an Iraqi city.

Chapter 18

GATHERING MOMENTUM: BEYOND THE SURGE

The autumn of 2007 brought with it the need to begin planning for the drawdown of U.S. forces, which would have to commence in mid-2008. Some of the brigades that had been on the ground when the surge began were already approaching the end of their 15-month tours, and even the surge forces themselves were due to begin redeploying over the winter. Both army and marine units faced the same situation. Moving them out while the insurgency was yet highly capable was a difficult undertaking. Petraeus did not want to reverse any gains that had been achieved. With the demand for forces remaining about the same, Petraeus knew that it had again become necessary to give the Iraqi Security Forces (ISF) a chance to backfill U.S. troops. He and Odierno began preaching to their tactical leaders that Coalition troops would "thin out, not hand off" as the ISF would augment the Coalition security presence on the ground. By the end of the year, the ISF had reached a strength of 200,000, an increase of 55 percent for the year, helped along by a massive infusion of equipment donated by the United States, including 6,000 high-mobility multi-wheeled vehicles (HMMWVs). Keeping the ISF in the field, for the foreseeable future, would still be a delicate balancing act.

In December, the UN Security Council approved Resolution 1790, extending the charter for the U.S. occupation for one more year. Maliki's government was not publicly in favor, because the Iraqis were increasingly eager to be seen as independent of the Americans. Maliki knew that his political future required that he be able to rule autonomously. When Iraq gained its independence, in the 1920s, Baghdad had allowed itself to remain a puppet of the British and had undermined its own credibility locally and in the region. Maliki vowed not to repeat that mistake. At the same time, he knew that terrorists remained a threat and that security was far too fragile for the ISF to handle on its own yet.

Demonstrating political reform was thus a priority. On January 12, 2008, the Council of Representatives took a step forward by passing the Justice and Accountability Act, formally outlawing the Baath Party and providing a path for reconciliation. The next month, it approved a provincial powers law calling for elections to be held by October, an amnesty law that specified how those who had served the former regime or fought against the central government could rehabilitate themselves, and a budget for the forthcoming year. Altogether, these amounted to a significant demonstration that normal political processes were returning to Iraq.

Petraeus began to think that while sectarian tensions remained volatile, it might be that Al Qaeda may have suffered so many setbacks inside of Iraq that with every further attack, they simply exposed their networks and bomb-making cells to destruction by U.S. forces. More and more information was arriving to the Coalition from Iraqis fed up with the violence and eager to see the perpetrators detained. To reassure a still impatient Congress, President Bush and Secretary Gates began venturing public conjecture that progress in Iraq could result in further reductions in Iraq later in 2008. But these two senior leaders also made it clear that Iraq remained a priority and that any drawdown would be predicated by conditions on the ground and the assessments provided by military commanders. These discussions about force sizing took a backseat when Maliki abruptly launched an offensive in Basra against the Jaysh al-Mahdi (JAM) militias there. Petraeus was only given short notice, and U.S. forces were not fully postured to support the ISF, which would lead the operation.

When the ISF struck, JAM fighters came out in force, and sharp street combat ensued in Basra. In Baghdad, JAM militias launched a furious rocket and mortar assault against the Green Zone. But this time, the ISF demonstrated that indeed it had improved. The ISF still needed extensive U.S. logistical, communications, air, and reconnaissance assistance, but it stayed and fought, supported by U.S. airpower in Basra and ground forces in Baghdad, all overseen by Odierno's successor, Lieutenant General Lloyd Austin. The favorable cease-fire that was negotiated after this tough fighting saw JAM's military power broken. The extortion rackets that JAM cells had been operating in Basra were taken down, and Maliki emerged with his stature greatly enhanced. In Baghdad, numerous JAM weapon caches were uncovered. Thus Maliki, a Shia, had shown his mettle as an Iraqi nationalist by attacking a Shia militia that opposed the central government. What would have prompted a crisis a year or two earlier now served to show the progress, both in political and military terms, that Iraq was making. There was satisfaction to take in this turn of events, although long-term challenges were still plentiful.

One major issue that neither Petraeus nor Iraqi leaders were able to fully assuage was the matter of Arab-Kurd relations. The progress achieved to date overall in Iraq notwithstanding, tensions between the two peoples and their respective political parties remained a contentious issue with the potential to erupt in new and major violence.

Since the U.S. invasion in 2003, Kurdish armed forces, known as *peshmerga*, had moved across the internal boundary known as the Green Line that delineated the territory controlled from Iraq's central government in Baghdad and that was administered by the Kurds. It was a semiautonomous area, one that Petraeus had long insisted that Kurdish leaders formally and publicly acknowledge as a part of Iraq. Petraeus reminded them repeatedly that there is only one Iraq. The Kurds knew this and, with varying degrees of sympathy, did agree that they were Iraqis first. However, this didn't stop them from sometimes raising the Iraqi state flag over their government buildings only when Petraeus or another U.S. general visited and promptly running up the Kurdish flag again when they departed.

While the *peshmerga* added welcome security in Ninewa, Kirkuk, and Diyala provinces, all in Iraqi-proper territory, their continued presence there caused increasing concern in Baghdad. Maliki and his allies had sought to strengthen the central government, limiting the authority of provincial governments and the Kurdish Regional Government (KRG). To make the point that he was not pleased with the Kurdish incursions, on several occasions, Maliki deployed Iraqi army units in close proximity to Kurdish formations. Such incidents necessitated hurried and aggressive responses from U.S. leaders on the ground to prevent escalations. While Petraeus, and then later Odierno, communicated directly with senior Iraqi officials, their commanders devised solutions at the tactical level, such as joining *peshmerga* and Iraqi security teams, conducting shared planning, and exchanging liaison officers. For their part, Kurdish officials repeatedly expressed concerns with what they viewed as Maliki's aspirations to consolidate power. Thus, they have pushed equally hard for expanded authority, territory, and resources to fulfill their ambition that the Kurdish people eventually become strong enough to resist any strong-arm tactics that could again emerge from either Baghdad or a neighboring country.

As both the government in Baghdad and the Kurds in the north wanted U.S. approval for their side, Multi-National Forces Iraq (MNF-I) and the U.S. embassy were able to wield decisive influence to promote accommodation and ensure that relations between Arabs and Kurds did not become violent. All sides knew, however, that the festering tensions remained a source of instability that could still rip apart the fabric of Iraqi society. For the time being then, Arab-Kurd tensions would have to be managed, rather than resolved.

Reconciliation with factions that opposed the Coalition had long been a hallmark of Petraeus's overall strategy in Iraq. Not every insurgent could, or should, be killed; ways had to be found to convince most to rejoin society. As Petraeus frequently noted, "You can't kill or capture your way out of an industrial-strength insurgency."[1] Although he had attempted modest reconciliation efforts in northern Iraq years before, it was while he was MNF-I commander that he institutionalized reconciliation as a key plank in the U.S. platform, initially taking considerable risk in doing so, given questions by Prime Minister Maliki and even from many within MNF-I. In doing so, he took as an example the progress that had been made in Anbar Province, dating back to 2005. There, Al Qaeda murders and intimidation prompted a group of 11 tribal sheikhs to oppose the group. While most of the tribal leaders were subsequently killed, their refusal to condone the terrorists' violence caught the public's attention and created the opportunity for marine and army forces in the region to reach out to the tribes. In time, more than 30 tribes agreed to begin policing their territory, in cooperation with the United States. This movement, dubbed the Anbar Awakening, ultimately totaled almost 20,000 Sunni men, who were paid by the United States to provide intelligence, search for weapons caches, rebuild police stations, and perform other civic duties. While attacks remained relatively high through 2006, by the middle of 2007, there was only about one a day in Anbar Province.

That same summer, about 15,000 Iraqis, who became known as the Sons of Iraq (SoI), in or near Baghdad had also agreed to serve their communities. These men too were largely Sunnis who had been alienated by the mayhem that had engulfed their neighborhoods and who realized that they must become more active or they would lose everything. Of course, this alarmed Maliki and other Shia leaders, who feared that an armed Sunni force would simply turn against the ISF and themselves. While Maliki was willing to allow the Anbar Awakening to develop in the Sunni lands of Anbar, the capital was another matter entirely. Petraeus established an elaborate process by which the Iraqi government could interview each applicant. Each potential SoI was photographed, fingerprinted, and screened to ensure that criminals were excluded. Given the harried nature of Iraqi administrative practices, this process was by no means full proof, but it did establish a fundamental level of credibility for the SoI. Under strict conditions, Maliki agreed to let the SoI serve in Baghdad. All SoI patrols had to be conducted only when ISF were also present; there could be no heavy weapons, and in Shia neighborhoods, there had to be some Shia SoI who also participated. Looking forward, Maliki promised that the government would hire about 25 percent into the police force over the next two years. The rest would be allowed to apply for positions elsewhere in a nonsecurity-related ministry.

Petraeus believed that this was a viable agreement, and SoI recruitment proceeded, with the numbers swelling to more than 100,000 across Iraq, primarily in the north, west, and around and within Baghdad. He viewed the engagement by local men who were willing to stand up to the insurgents as a way to strengthen the ties between local communities and the central government. As long as factions were talking, stability was fostered. Now reconciliation on other fronts was also proving fruitful.

After much pressing by Petraeus and his lieutenants at MNF-I, Maliki agreed to allow members of Saddam Hussein's army who still lived inside of Iraq to apply for a pension and rights as professional military members. Otherwise, this group of experienced military men was prone to be disruptive, and their skills were in great demand by the insurgents. Outreach to them was a way to counter this tendency. Petraeus had found previously that difficult economic times and a desire by these soldiers to restore their honor would tempt many to seek legitimate accommodation. As expected, Maliki's outreach prompted more than 110,000 men to register with the government at 11 centers across Iraq. After reviewing their files, the government accepted 7,000 for return to duty with the Iraqi army and another 70,000 to receive the much-desired pensions.

Of even greater consequence were the outreach efforts toward the SoI. With U.S. money to provide salaries to the SoI running out and little inclination in Washington to renew funding, it was imperative that the Iraqi government pay them or risk alienating the SoI. The government had formerly agreed to employ all of the SoI, but implementation had been lagging. Now prodded by U.S. leaders, Maliki consented. As with former regime soldiers, the first step was to identify the SoI and then to officially transfer them to the government so they could be given jobs and receive state funds. The goal was to hire formally about 20 percent of the SoI into Iraq's security services and to place the remaining members in other government agencies, such as the Ministry of Agriculture and Education. By mid-2009, this had largely been accomplished, even if some of the jobs were of a temporary nature. Petraeus and Odierno could, however, look upon this aspect of reconciliation with satisfaction—the SoI, an ally of the United States during the height of the insurgency and made up mostly of Sunnis, had been reintegrated into government organizations that were mostly Shia led. This was not an insignificant feat.

Reconciliation with groups that persisted to act violently provided a different sort of problem. There was virtually no room for accommodation with Al Qaeda fighters, but some channels did exist through Maliki's government to reach out to hostile Shia groups. These negotiations were led by Iraqis and went forward cautiously. The talks began with the premise that all fighters must declare a formal cease-fire, turn in weapons, and declare a willingness to return to legitimate, peaceful political processes. In return, the government of Iraq was to provide income and jobs to members of the group and facilitate the release of detainees in U.S. or Iraqi custody. It was a difficult, uncomfortable, and necessary approach justified only because of the overwhelming need to return peace to Iraq.

Surprisingly, many of the insurgents came to see the Americans as neutral and objective participants who stood outside of the passions of Iraqi political competition and so could be trusted to render fair judgments. As such, MNF-I was able to keep the reconciliation process moving. It was one more way that U.S. leaders had learned to wage a counterinsurgency campaign. Like all sides in Iraq, the Americans had come a long way since 2003. But despite these many steps, Petraeus knew much yet needed to be done. Many individuals on both sides remained skeptical of the entire undertaking, and mutual suspicion persisted. As with so much in Iraq, reconciliation was a tool in the kit bag to be used judiciously, and just one of many needed to repair the country's long-neglected organs of civil and political life.

While political and military activities usually took center stage, Petraeus devoted nearly equal attention to restoring Iraq's economic vitality. Iraqis needed funds to rebuild their society, without which they would remain discouraged and vulnerable. Iraqis themselves knew this full well and began to speak up. In 2008, junior officers began to report that they were seeing a notable change in the priorities of Iraqis emerging. For the first time since U.S. troops had arrived, Iraqis were telling the Americans that government services and economic opportunity were foremost in their minds. Security was still a major concern, but it no longer stood alone as an urgent matter for Iraqis.

As Petraeus noted to his staff on many occasions, no single factor would go as far toward reestablishing prosperity in Iraq as much as dependable power to light Iraqi homes and run Iraqi businesses. Since 2004, the United States had spent about $4 billion to help rebuild Iraq's power production and distribution system, but progress had been uneven from month to month. It was not until 2007 that production had reached about 4,000 megawatts, roughly the same as it had been prior to the invasion. Coalition projects, such as MNF-I's extensive effort to shepherd enormous engines in cumbersome convoys lumbering across Iraq from Jordan, destined to operate a power plant in Samarra, were finally coming online and beginning to pay off. In 2008, power topped 5,000 megawatts. He drove his energy team to help the Iraqis do better, and the next year, it would top 6,700 megawatts.

But even though output was increasing, so was the demand for power. The U.S. embassy estimated that only about 65 percent of Iraq's electricity requirements were being met. And power generation wasn't the only challenge; transmission and distribution of power was also a problem. As a result, the average Iraqi could expect to turn on the lights only about 16 hours a day; some areas received as few as 3 hours of power a day.

To increase the flow of commercial goods and foster economic growth, MNF-I undertook several initiatives to upgrade the Iraqis' transportation architecture. In the winter of 2009, several principle projects met with success. With U.S. supervision, the Iraqi national railroad moved two trains of 40 containers from central Iraq to the port at Umm Qasr in the south. Also, building upon a program that had been growing for several years, MNF-I continued to contract with the Iraq Transportation Network (ITN), a consortium of tribally owned truck companies that have gained expertise moving U.S. military cargo. Initially focused primarily in central and northern Iraq, MNF-I was now extending the ITN's reach to the southern provinces. The ITN was another way to build Iraqi commercial experience.

Of course, Petraeus was also keenly aware of the critical role that oil production and export needed to play in Iraq's reconstruction. From his early efforts to reopen the oil trade with Syria while he commanded in Mosul, Petraeus had been directly involved in this historic issue. Like many Middle Eastern states, the discovery of large quantities of oil during the 1920s and 1930s in Iraq dramatically altered its place in the international economy. With the return of foreign oil companies after World War II, many of them American, the lifeblood of the region has been oil. This has certainly been the case for Iraq. More than 90 percent of the nation's gross domestic product comes from its export. Iraq's proven oil reserves of 112 billion barrels ranks it among the world's richest. And vast tracts of Iraq remain unsurveyed for additional reserves, which could total as much as another 100 billion barrels.

The extensive damages inflicted during the insurgency meant that restarting and accelerating oil production had proved an enormous challenge. The war had added to the misery experienced by Iraq's oil industry, which had been suffering for nearly 20 years already. Shortly after its failed 1990 invasion of Kuwait and the imposition of resulting trade embargoes, Iraq's oil production fell from more than 3 million barrels per day to about 300,000 barrels per day. More than a decade later, on the eve of the U.S. invasion, Iraqi oil production had mostly recovered, and officials at the time were hoping to increase the country's oil production capacity even further but could not do so due to the already faltering technical conditions of its oil fields, pipelines, and other related infrastructure. Now, after more years of neglect, technical obsolescence, and a long war during which insurgents frequently targeted the energy sector, the oil industry was in shambles.

As a consequence, government revenues had taken a hit, constraining nearly all rebuilding efforts. Iraq had been earning about $11 billion in revenue in 2002 (most of it stolen by Saddam Hussein and his cronies), but far less than that since. To a great degree, declining production had been offset by the rapid rise of oil prices on the international market that had pushed national revenues to as high as $60 billion in 2008. But with the onset of the worldwide recession, forecasts for 2009 and beyond were for a level less than half of that. The result was a projected budget deficit of some $20 billion, forcing the government to make difficult decisions about how to make trade-offs between funding security and nonsecurity needs.

Unfortunately, there were few short-term remedies. Iraq's minister of oil, Husayn al-Shahristani, had been seeking to attract investment by international oil companies, and interest had been building. Many, however, remained reluctant to commit to Iraq due to confusion over the contracting process and persistent security fears. Experts had concluded that with substantial investment and upgrades, Iraq could achieve within a decade a sustainable production capacity—probably about 2.5 to 3 million barrels per day, although the government had set an ambitious target of 12 million barrels per day. But even if foreign oil contracts were obtained, significant production increases (especially in the southern oil fields) were no doubt years away.

Every day at the morning update, Petraeus devoured data about the critical oil sector. He daily peppered his energy experts, named the Energy Fusion Cell and led by UK officers with extensive experience in the energy sector, with question after question to ensure that MNF-I was doing all it could to facilitate the Iraqis' efforts. He knew that the first and best thing the Americans could do was to ensure that military protection was sufficient to allow this civilian-led aspect of Iraq's economy to resurrect itself. There had been about 400 insurgent attacks against oil refineries and distribution assets since 2003. Hence he prioritized oil-related security operations and outreach, whether that was pursuing Al

Qaeda extortion networks in the northern fields, guarding pipeline re-construction, or making introductions for the Iraqis to U.S. experts.

Oil was another sore point between the Kurds and Baghdad. Several oil fields in the north had been refurbished, and the Kurds were about to begin flowing oil, some of it through Turkey. Maliki, of course, wanted a percentage of the revenue to go to Baghdad's coffers, rightly pointing out that oil from the Kurdish regions was still Iraqi oil. Negotiations were proceeding. In the south, about 800 sailors from American and UK naval task forces had been securing Iraq's two offshore oil terminals in the Per-sian Gulf for years. These terminals were essential for the export of Iraqi crude to world markets. It was about all Americans could do. Renewed ef-forts to grow other private industries to diversify the Iraqi economy were underway also, but it would be years before Iraq saw measurable benefits. Oil would be the name of the game as Iraq rebuilt, and there were limits to U.S. military power, Petraeus knew. Oil was the property of the Iraqis, and it was ultimately up to them to revive their greatest natural re-source.

It seemed evident that by the summer of 2008, the tide of war that had swept over Iraq since 2003 had begun to recede. The fight in Basra had been largely won. Operations in the rest of the country were proceeding without setbacks. Governance was gradually improving, and the econ-omy was at least not getting worse. Petraeus, the fresh troops of the surge, the Anaconda strategy, and COIN precepts had achieved what appeared to be sustainable momentum. The war was not over by any means, but for the near term at least, U.S. and Coalition forces had finally created space for the Iraqi government at all levels to rebuild itself. In America, the sense of alarm that had saturated the media airwaves and political corridors of Washington had likewise subsided. All the shrill talk about another Vietnam simply evaporated.

By the fall, Petraeus was ready for a change of scenery. He was tired, but he was also ready to test himself on a bigger playing field. For a time, it had seemed like he was destined for assignment to command U.S. forces in Europe, which would have been a good fit for him. Holly's fa-ther had been posted there after he departed West Point, as had Jack Galvin, Petraeus's mentor. In addition, he and Holly had enjoyed their previous tours there. But when Admiral Fallon had abruptly resigned in the spring, largely due to his disagreement with Washington regarding the conduct of the war in Iraq and critical comments about the Bush administration to reporters, the calculations in the Pentagon regarding senior officer assignments changed. Instead of Europe, Petraeus would go to Tampa, Florida, and take command at the headquarters of U.S. Central Command, or CENTCOM.

All the while, Holly kept together the Petraeus army family. Like many a military wife, she could state proudly, "I've never lived more than four years in one place."[2] Describing herself to a journalist, she chose the terms *self-sufficient* and *reliable*, apt words for a woman who held down the home front for 35 years of marriage. She was also active publicly. Since 2004, she had served as executive director of the Better Business Bureau's Military Line, a division that assists family members in being more financially responsible. And as advisor to the Children of Fallen Patriots Foundation, she "helps brainstorm how to raise visibility and funds to provide scholarships to children of servicemen who died in combat and in training."[3] Now she would be doing these things while her husband assumed even wider responsibilities. Even though he was going to be assigned to Tampa, it was almost certain he would spend little time there.

Despite the difficult combat conditions in Iraq, overall morale remained consistently high. Reenlistment ceremonies such as this 2007 event, held in Al Faw Palace at Camp Victory on the western outskirts of Baghdad, became a regular occurrence. On July 4, 2008, Petraeus reenlisted more than 1,200 troops in a single event at Al Faw. AP Photo/Kim Gamel.

CENTCOM is one of the 10 major commands that the Pentagon assigns responsibility for preparing or deploying America's military operations around the world. Four of the commands have functional responsibilities, such as transportation, planning, and training. Six of them, including CENTCOM, are tasked to supervise military operations in a specified part of the world. CENTCOM's area of responsibility, or AOR, includes 20 nations of the Middle East, and Petraeus would be in charge of more than 200,000 soldiers, sailors, airmen, marines, and coast guardsmen serving on active duty in the region. With much larger scope, he would not only oversee military affairs, but would also be involved in questions of military basing and posture, working alongside the Department of State to foster better relations with the countries of the region, and, of course, with America's other active war in the region—Afghanistan. But, of course, critical events in Iraq were still underway, and from his new position, Petraeus continued to be involved. Iraq had become his investment. He had made every bet and would see it through to the end.

NOTES

1. Colleen Walsh, "General Petraeus Talks of Lessons Learned, Challenges Ahead," *Harvard News Office*, April 22, 2009, http://www. hks.harvard.edu/news-events/news/articles/petreaus-cpl-forum-apr09.

2. Amy Scherzer, "General's Wife Getting to Know Tampa," *St. Petersburg Times*, May 24, 2009, http://www.tampabay.com/news/ military/macdill/article1003733.ece.

3. Ibid.

Chapter 19

THE U.S. ENDGAME
IN IRAQ

As the arrival of a new year approached, the sixth since the invasion of Iraq in 2003, the calendar brought with it the promise of significant strategic change in Iraq. While the ongoing work to maintain pressure on both Shia and Sunni insurgents, and the simultaneous efforts to improve governance and training of the Iraqi Security Forces (ISF), would continue, there were larger developments afoot: the governments of Iraq and the United States were on the verge of implementing a new diplomatic arrangement; Iraqi provincial elections were scheduled to occur; and in November, the United States would hold a presidential election. Each of these was a watershed event that would influence Iraq's fortune and would go far to color the American as well as regional and international views of Iraq. From his position as overall U.S. commander for the region, Petraeus's job was to ensure that Odierno had the resources he needed to sustain the positive trajectory inside the country. Both men fully knew that America's stake in Iraq could still come undone even at this stage, and they were committed to seeing their mission through.

Both publicly and privately, Petraeus and Odierno each emphasized the rather remarkable fact that the situation in Iraq had improved far enough both in terms of security gains and stabilizing political structures to permit consideration of new approaches, all of which pointed to the departure of foreign troops from Iraqi soil. Normalcy still lay in the future, but for the first time, a genuine hope for Iraq's eventual reintegration in the community of nations as a regional partner and a belief that its people could enjoy peace and prosperity began to be felt by Iraqis and Americans alike. It was a fragile conviction, but that it could take shape at all was a sign of the tremendous progress already achieved.

The first day of January 2009 saw two new military and diplomatic agreements take hold, foreshadowing this important year of transitions. On the diplomatic front, the departure or announced end of participation by all Coalition partners except the United States, and the expiration at the end of 2008 of the UN Security Council Resolution (UNSCR) 1790 that had governed the presence of Coalition forces inside of Iraq, meant that follow-on arrangements had to be negotiated. The result was two new arrangements that were to define and describe the relationship between the United States and Iraq.

The Security Agreement (known informally as the SA; its full title is *Agreement Between the United States of America and the Republic of Iraq on the Withdrawal of United States Forces from Iraq and the Organization of Their Activities during Their Temporary Presence in Iraq*) defines the rules governing the presence of U.S. forces in Iraq through 2011. In short, the SA established a series of joint Iraq-U.S. committees to regulate how U.S. forces would conduct operations in Iraq. Although a cumbersome and complex arrangement, and one the Iraqis initially struggled to get up and running, the SA would prove over time an effective method of fostering communication and coordination between leaders at all levels and one that was approached in good faith.

A second agreement, a nonbinding Strategic Framework Agreement, or SFA (full title: *Strategic Framework Agreement for a Relationship of Friendship and Cooperation between the United States of America and the Republic of Iraq*), outlined the principles for ongoing economic, diplomatic, cultural, and security cooperation between the United States and Iraq. The SFA pointed to the creation of a long-term relationship and in so doing planted the seed for an enduring partnership that would be addressed more fully in the future. However, with the SFA, the precedent for a unique relationship between Iraq and the United States was officially sanctioned, even if both governments for the time being found it politically convenient not to speak too forthrightly about it.

In dramatic fashion, the implementation of the SA and SFA influenced the operating environment for American forces inside of Iraq. These agreements certified that restoration of Iraq's full sovereignty as a nation-state and meant that going forward, American forces were the guests of the government of Iraq, a subtle but key distinction and a sign that the United States was on the path to withdrawal. Reflective of the evolving conditions, Petraeus had turned to his staff to publish a refreshed Joint Campaign Plan, or JCP, shortly before he changed command in September. In partnership with the diplomatic team in the U.S. embassy, Odierno had subsequently revised the JCP more thoroughly in November and December. This JCP was an essential document that outlined the framework used by the Multi-National Forces Iraq (MNF-I) for implementing all operations in Iraq, whether they be military, political, economic, or diplomatic. It would also serve as the baseline for the recommendations that Petraeus and Odierno would make later in the winter to President Obama regarding the future of America's involvement in Iraq.

In late July 2008, presidential candidate Barack Obama, left, visited Iraq for the first time. General Petraeus conducted a helicopter tour over Baghdad to demonstrate firsthand the progress that was then underway to dampen violence and achieve U.S. objectives. AP Photo/Ssg. Lorie Jewell, HO.

In practical terms, as the Iraqis seized more and more of the daily decision making regarding what was happening within their borders, from security operations to mail service, both the Iraqi government and U.S. military headquarters in Baghdad needed to devise systems to define and regulate their authorities. Initially, this was to occur formally through the SA's committee structure, and informally through the near-daily conversations and meetings between Odierno and his key leaders and Prime Minister Maliki and his advisors, as well as Iraq's president, two vice presidents, and leaders in the Council of Representatives. At the same time, civilian leaders on both sides would increasingly make more and more of the decisions as the security continued to improve. This meant that Odierno not only expected but endorsed a higher-profile role for Ambassador Hill and his team in Baghdad. While the top levels of authority were working cooperatively, MNF-I was to continue to assist the Iraqis to improve their delivery of basic services to the Iraqi people and provide an overall better level of governance. Finally, the JCP, envisioned that the growing strategic partnership between Iraq and the United States would lead to even further protocols to enable their relations to mutual strategic benefit.

One of the soonest and most visible manifestations of the new conditions was the transfer of control of property from U.S. forces to Iraqi authorities. Crocker, Odierno, and Maliki agreed that the place to symbolically demonstrate Iraq's returning independence was Baghdad's International Zone (IZ). Thus, at a heavily guarded New Year's Day ceremony, the government of Iraq publicly welcomed back the return of the Republican Palace, Iraq's former seat of government that had been occupied by MNF-I in the IZ since shortly after the invasion. Several weeks later, MNF-I presented a list of almost 400 facilities across the country that the United States was to return as soon as arrangements could be made. On the list were installations occupied by military units as small as a few dozen soldiers, all the way up to those hosting thousands.

The closure or return of U.S.-occupied facilities was a visible sign of America's compliance with the Security Agreement and growing Iraqi sovereignty. Petraeus was pleased, and when making his rounds of Washington's media outlets, he reiterated that he continued to be guardedly confident. Soon his faith would be tested, as Iraqis faced another critical event domestically, the holding of provincial elections, a matter of great political urgency and another signpost that would indicate the degree that Iraqis and their leaders could, or would, tolerate the emotions that were an inevitable component of unconstrained political competition.

These elections were to populate the government councils of Iraq's provinces, thereby setting the stage for national elections in 2010 and serving as a barometer for the strength of the various parties and factions vying for power and influence. There were 440 seats at stake, with more than 14,000 candidates running, including nearly 4,000 women, a rather unprecedented feat for a Middle Eastern state. Another unique feature of the law was that it directed that religious minorities be represented, even if in small numbers. For example, in Baghdad Province, 1 seat was allocated for Christians and another for Mandaean Sabians. In Ninewa, a single position was allocated for each of the Christian, Shabak, and Yazidi minorities. And in Basra, Christians were allocated 1 seat on the council.

Originally, elections had been slated to be held in mid-2008 but had been pushed back several times due to the wrangling over the enabling law in the Council of Representatives. When the law was ratified in October with a provision that the election occur no later than the end of January 2009, it was met with great relief, but through the late autumn, Petraeus and Odierno had been concerned that elections would be delayed due to political quarrelling in Baghdad. U.S. leaders also remained concerned that the Iraqi High Electoral Commission, the body overseeing the election, would be unable to support them in time, but with close and sustained U.S. assistance, the Iraqis kept to their announced timeline. On the American side, President Obama's election in November caused some Iraqis to question the U.S. commitment to Iraq, but Petraeus and Odierno provided reassurances that the United States remained steadfast. They foresaw a strategic review being undertaken by the new administration after it was inaugurated in mid-January, but believed that the Iraqi government had many solid reasons to believe the United States would sustain its support, and in any case, the elections were critical for upholding the government of Iraq's legitimacy.

From start to finish, the electoral process was run by Iraqis, although MNF-I accommodated the United Nations, which led the international community's oversight. The United Nations certified observers to certify voter lists, monitored polling places, and tracked the completed ballots until they could be certified. In all, 77 international organizations and a score of diplomatic missions were present for the election. During the run-up to election day, about 15 million voters registered to cast ballots in 14 of Iraq's 18 provinces. (Elections in the Kurdistan region and the still-violent province of Tamim were to be postponed.)

For the first time in Iraq's history, campaign posters appeared, papered to light poles and concrete blast barriers across the major cities. Candidates who ultimately won largely emphasized the need for better government services, the importance of modern financial accounting, and governmental reform. Notably, and reflective of U.S. achievements in Iraq, was as sharp nationalist tone from candidates who wanted to distance Iraq from Iranian influence. This new tone was picked up by the regional media, and those parties that relied upon sectarian identity to attract adherents, largely lost support.

To forestall election-related violence, ISF worked closely with MNF-I to implement a number of security measures. Intelligence collection was stepped up, and proactive security operations uncovered bomb-making and insurgent cells. Overall levels of violence in the weeks preceding the vote remained low, and while there were several election-related assassinations and attacks on political offices and polling sites, including the assassination of six candidates in Ninewa, Diyala, Babil, and Baghdad provinces, the Iraqi public was not deterred from participating.

On January 31st, nearly 7 million Iraqis safely voted at the more than 6,000 polling sites. Only two attacks were reported. A few mortars landed near a polling site in the city of Tikrit, and a polling station in Mosul was shot at, but there were no casualties reported in either attack. Slightly less than 50 percent of eligible voters turned out to vote, a rate lower than Petraeus had hoped for, but a welcome number nonetheless, given the significant challenges that had to be overcome, including a complex voter-registration system that was tied to the public's receipt of ration cards. Curfews and vehicle bans, which were instituted to improve security, may have also had the unanticipated consequence of preventing some Iraqis from reaching the polls. These were lessons noted for the future, but for the present, Iraq's first truly open, nationwide elections had been accomplished.

When the votes were tallied several weeks later, Prime Minister Maliki's coalition performed better than expected, winning a plurality of seats in nine southern provinces and Baghdad, a further indicator of the public's general endorsement of the path laid out for the U.S.-Iraq relationship by Generals Petraeus and Odierno, and Ambassador Hill. Notably, the elections helped correct the domestic disparities in the provinces that stemmed from the boycott by many Sunnis during elections in 2005, particularly in the western and central provinces. The new balance heralded an important shift in the political landscape and suggested that Iraq was at least approaching sustainable governance.

Odierno and Petraeus each often commented that the success of a new representative government wasn't whether it could hold a single election; whether it could do so a second time was the true measure that democratic institutions were taking hold. Thus proved to be the case in Iraq. Even if secular political reform was relatively novel and yet tenuous, it had proved to be viable. From his headquarters in Tampa, Petraeus could see that the provincial elections marked yet another watershed moment for the United States and Iraq. Although the attention of the Iraq-fatigued American media and public were consumed with the deepening recession and political theater of a new presidency and so gave the event only passing mention, the results demonstrated in clear terms that the Iraqi body politic was moving in a direction toward greater inclusiveness and moderation, a promising outcome after years of insurgency and extremism. The next major electoral challenge for Iraq would be national parliamentary elections to be held in March 2010. U.S. support had already been ongoing for months, and Petraeus and Odierno were guardedly optimistic that the Iraqis would perform just as well as they had this time.

As security improved and as Iraq's economic potential was again recognized internationally, Iraq accelerated its efforts to revitalize relationships with its neighbors, a process that Petraeus worked on hard from CENTCOM. Saddam Hussein's invasion of Kuwait and his blustering posture on the diplomatic stage long intimidated fellow Arab states, but they began warming to Iraq in late 2008 and into 2009. Prospects for bilateral cooperation in a variety of areas, including infrastructure, tourism, agricultural development, and investment, began to be increasingly discussed by officials in the Ministry of Foreign Affairs. Iraq's participation in events such as the inaugural Arab Economic Summit in early 2009 began to build Iraq's credibility. The summit, which was held in Kuwait, drew participation from all of the Arab League states. Bilateral meetings between Iraqi and Kuwaiti representatives were also held during the conference to address long-standing grievances from the Gulf War. Separate visits by French president Nicholas Sarkozy and the German foreign minister signaled growing diplomatic ties between Iraq and those two countries. Visiting delegations from Japan, China, South Korea, and other Asian nations were also soon underway.

Despite these positive diplomatic signs, several potentially destabilizing aspects of Iraq's diplomatic relations remained problematic. This was particularly the case with regard to Iran. Iraq's leadership maintains close ties with Iran and frequently travels to Tehran for meetings. As Shias who were persecuted by Saddam Hussein, many of Iraq's leading government officials have lifelong ties to their Iranian counterparts since they sought refuge there or in Shia communities elsewhere in the region. Time and again, Petraeus encouraged Maliki and his advisors to pursue a relationship with Iran that was beneficial to Iraq, while limiting Iran's destabilizing influences, which is not easy to do as long as Iran's leadership continues to seek to entrench and extend its influence inside of Iraq. As Iraq's main trading partner, Iran has invested heavily in Iraq's essential service infrastructure, religious tourism, and housing sectors. This investment is badly needed and has led to quality-of-life improvements, particularly in southern Iraq. However, during provincial elections, Iran also funds political candidates and parties whose loyalty to Tehran likely trumps that to Baghdad, and it still provides a refuge to some insurgents who have fled the ISF and the United States.

Petraeus was also involved with other diplomatic initiatives related to Iraq. For instance, the governments of Turkey, Iraq, and the United States have participated in diplomatic talks aimed at synchronizing political, military, and economic approaches to regional problems. These discussions include information sharing, particularly in advance of Turkish military strikes aimed at Kurdish separatist groups that operate on both sides of the Turkish-Iraqi border. These groups use the rugged terrain in the area as refuge. Progress was made as the Iraqi government increasingly insisted that Turkey respect its sovereignty, and the Turks supported the principle of more transparent cooperation.

As part of a broader effort led from Washington to broaden America's approach to Middle Eastern states, Petraeus and CENTCOM monitored overtures to Syria, another state that was also warming toward Iraq. Syria appointed an ambassador to Iraq in late 2009, its first since 1979, and in January, Iraq reciprocated. Petraeus watched these developments carefully as Syria's cooperation would go far toward both stabilizing Iraq and serving as a valuable brake to slow Iranian ambitions. Both U.S. and Iraqi leaders continued to be concerned with reports that Syria was not doing all it could to tighten its border security and that there might be Al Qaeda–related fighters migrating through Syria to Iraq. Prime Minister Maliki's government held out to the Syrians the possibility of reviving economic links, especially a pipeline to carry oil from Iraq's north to the Syrian port of Baniyas on the Mediterranean. Such an arrangement held clear benefits to both states; before the U.S. invasion, the pipeline carried several hundred thousand barrels of oil per day. It was as if Petraeus's early adventures to open a pipeline while commanding in Mosul had finally come to fruition.

Another high-profile issue that Petraeus and Odierno had to work on carefully was the issue of detainee operations. Once the SA took effect, U.S. forces were no longer allowed to keep the thousands of Iraqi prisoners still being held; all detainees had to be under Iraqi control and court jurisdiction. MNF-I was thus transitioning the legacy detainee population. This was to be done by transferring them to Iraqi custody for prosecution in Iraqi courts on criminal charges or by releasing them from detention in a safe and orderly manner in accordance with the Geneva convention. A challenge presented itself, however, from the fact that the Iraqi authorities were not ready to receive such a large number of detainees. The Iraqi court system was cumbersome and slow, and its jails were overcrowded. There was thus a high probability that many prisoners would simply be released, and there was a concern that transferred detainees might not receive adequate protections within the Iraqi system. The solution devised by the United States was to assess the detainees in terms of their likelihood to commit further acts of violence in the future. It was certainly an inexact science, but by modulating the flow of releases, U.S. officers could best ensure that prisoners received just treatment while the worst offenders were kept in jail until their cases could be fully administered.

While these political and diplomatic events were underway, military operations were proceeding, aimed primarily at defeating Al Qaeda in Iraq (AQI) and other extremists in Mosul and in Ninewa Province, and to disrupt traditional smuggling routes in western Iraq. To help these efforts, U.S. training was stepped up to professionalize the Iraqi Department of Border Enforcement (DBE) for the purpose of reducing corruption at points of entry (POE) along the border with Syria and Jordan. In the south, U.S. and ISF units partnered to interdict lethal aid being smuggled from Iran and conducted tribal engagements to deepen relations between the southern provinces and Baghdad. These military operations were some of the final combined operations that the United States and ISF would perform together. In June, per the mandates of the SA, all U.S. combat forces were to be withdrawn from Iraq's cities. It would be a momentous occasion, as it signaled the maturation of the ISF and of Maliki's government, whose aspirations to be independent of the Americans was now matched by a definite capacity to do so, at least to a modest degree. While Iraq still needed extensive U.S. support to control its airspace and to protect its oil terminals in the Persian Gulf, it could boast to the Iraqi public that its reforms were demonstrably resulting in a U.S. drawdown. And in fact that drawdown was indeed picking up speed.

Shortly after being inaugurated in January, President Obama asked his national security team to provide him with options for the withdrawal of U.S. forces from Iraq. MNF-I and CENTCOM prepared several courses of action for withdrawal, outlining the advantages and risks associated with each one. Senior officials in the Obama administration carefully considered these courses of action and weighed them against the force requirements in Afghanistan and elsewhere. On February 27th, President Obama announced that the U.S. combat mission in Iraq would end by August 31, 2010, in accordance with a 19-month withdrawal timeline. This plan called for the accelerated reduction of U.S. forces from 14 brigade combat teams to 6 advisory and assistance brigades by August 2010. After that point, a residual force of 35,000–50,000 U.S. troops would remain in Iraq on an interim basis to train, equip, and advise the ISF; to conduct targeted counterterrorism missions; and to protect remaining U.S. military and civilian assets. By the end of 2011, all U.S. forces would depart Iraq. While the SA was to expire at that point, the ongoing strategic partnership outlined in the Strategic Framework Agreement would endure. Polls indicated that Iraqis welcomed the president's plan, although they remained well aware of Iraq's enduring sectarian and political tensions. The future was growing brighter, but it would likely be a long time before the storm clouds that lingered over Iraq's domestic horizon could be made to disappear from view. In any case, the future would belong to the Iraqis now. They had a country, if the Sunnis and Shia and Kurds could dampen their individual ambitions and allow Iraqi nationalism to grow deep roots.

Perhaps the most favorable statistic for the United States came in December. Odierno, whose command had been extensively reorganized as United States Forces-Iraq (replacing MNF-I) to reflect the drawdown mission, reported that the month passed without a single service member being killed in combat. It was the first month since the invasion without a U.S. trooper being killed by hostile fire. Odierno reported that over the past two years, there had been a 92 percent decrease in security incidents, a 90 percent decrease in high-profile attacks, a 94 percent decrease in civilian casualties, and a 90 percent decrease in U.S. casualties. Petraeus noted at the same time that attacks against U.S. forces had dropped from more than 200 a day two years ago, to about 15 a day. As Petraeus said, "It's a time for reflection on past achievements and on the hard work that clearly still lies ahead."[1] This success had come at a terrible cost: more than 4,300 Americans had died in Iraq, and more than 31,000 had been treated for physical wounds. The number of service men and women who suffer from traumatic brain injuries resulting from blows to the head that are difficult to detect and quantify are unknown but probably amount to several thousand more. Those who suffer psychologically from varying degrees of posttraumatic stress disorder (PTSD), in the form of nightmares or difficulty adjusting to civilian routines, are much higher, no doubt in the tens of thousands. And military families have paid a price too. A study of 250,000 army wives, two-thirds whose husbands had fought in Iraq and Afghanistan between 2003 and 2006, revealed incidents of depression 18–24 percent higher than their civilian peers. It is no surprise that rates of prescription drug abuse are on the rise across the military. A young army captain, reflecting on the differences between the wars in the Middle East; World War II, when America's armed forces were kept full by a draft; and Vietnam, during which most soldiers and marines served one-year tours, stated: "My grandfathers' generation is always called the 'greatest generation.' I disagree. It's these men here [in Iraq and Afghanistan] who go to war three or four times and continue to do what's asked of them, when others refuse."[2]

Iraqis, of course, suffered the most. Iraqi deaths certainly totaled more than 85,000, with about 150,000 wounded and 2 million forced to flee their homes. In recognition of these losses, Petraeus addressed the Iraqi officers present, thanking them for their "tremendous courage and determination in the face of innumerable challenges, continuous threats and periodic tragic loss." Mindful of the service of his soldiers, and of the limits of a general in any battle, he addressed them directly: "You, our troopers, have been the single element in all that we have done in Iraq with our Iraqi brothers. You have been the ones who have translated concepts and ideas . . . into reality on the ground, under body armor and rucksack, in tough conditions, against an often barbaric enemy."[3] For the soldiers in attendance, there was little celebration. The troops knew they still had much work to do. For Petraeus and his soldiers alike, however, the changes that they had instituted in the dark days when Iraq was slipping into civil war were now vindicated. They had indeed overcome the naysayers at home and the insurgents in Iraq.

NOTES

1. Michael Hastings, "December First Month without U.S. Combat Death in Iraq," *WashingtonPost.com*, January 1, 2010, http://www.huff ingtonpost.com/2010/01/01/december-1st-month-withou_n_409013. html.

2. Gregg Zoroya, "Repeated Deployments Weigh Heavily On Troops," *USA Today.com*, January 13, 2010, http://www.usatoday.com/ news/military/2010-01-12-four-army-war-tours_N.htm.

3. "U.S. Forces: Iraq Stands Up in Baghdad," *Air Force News Service*, January 4, 2010, http://www.af.mil/news/story.asp?id=123184054.

Chapter 20

A NEW WAR IN AFGHANISTAN

While in Iraq the order of business was to draw down—a total of 31 million items to be packed up and shipped, including 43,000 military vehicles, 600 helicopters, 120,000 freight containers, and 34,000 tons of ammunition—in Afghanistan, forces were building up. U.S. forces had been in the country since late 2001, when they launched an assault that drove the ruling Taliban regime from power, killing many of their leaders and scattering the rest. The Taliban were Islamic extremists who had toppled a Communist puppet government installed after the Soviets retreated from the country in 1989, nine years after they invaded in a bid to incorporate Afghanistan into the Soviet orbit. The Taliban were ruthless administrators who imposed a harsh form of Islam and drove the already-impoverished nation further into despair. It was from within Afghanistan that Al Qaeda operated the training camps that harbored Osama bin Laden in the years preceding the September 11, 2001, terrorist attacks, and hence, it became America's chief target in the following months.

But since installing a pro-Western government in 2002, U.S. forces had operated in what became a secondary theater. The American commitment, formally organized under the auspices of NATO (North

Atlantic Treaty Organization), took a backseat to events elsewhere. Hence the military effort in Afghanistan languished, the resources available largely starved by the war in Iraq. By the time success began to appear in Iraq in 2008, the Taliban, which had been husbanding its strength, again burst onto the international scene with renewed vigor. It again attacked the central government and again seized control over substantial swaths of territory. The United States and its NATO allies could no longer afford to ignore the war in Afghanistan.

In the early spring of 2009, President Obama reaffirmed America's dedication to the struggle in Afghanistan and ordered more troops to deploy. Then, after a lengthy review of the overall strategy, he announced on December 1, 2009, from West Point that he was ordering an additional 30,000 combat forces to Afghanistan. He added that U.S forces would begin drawing down by July 2011, meaning that he expected Petraeus, as CENTCOM commander, and General Stanley McChrystal, responsible on the ground in Afghanistan, to demonstrate progress by that time. Petraeus knew full well that whatever was achieved by then would only be the first installment of a long campaign.

As the troops that had served in Iraq previously soon learned, duty in Afghanistan brought fresh challenges, some similar and some new. They were quick to point out to their leaders that while counterinsurgency, or COIN, tactics applied to each theater, Afghanistan offered a tough fight against a new kind of resilient enemy. One difference stemmed from the fact that Taliban fighters could seek refuge along the rugged terrain of the Afghanistan-Pakistan border.

Improvised explosive devices (IEDs), vehicle-borne bombs, and suicide attacks were common methods of attack, as they were in Iraq; but this time, the Taliban were able to hide among the wider population, especially in rural areas, in a broader fashion than insurgents in Iraq could do. While lacking the religious divides that marked Iraq's struggle (the Taliban are overwhelmingly Sunni, as are all Afghans), conflict in Afghanistan was often waged along tribal and clan lines; hence, U.S. and Coalition forces found themselves confronted with a sectarian war that they had to resolve.

When describing what U.S. forces were facing, Petraeus was candid about what he expected to lay ahead. As he told Congress in late 2009, "Achieving progress in Afghanistan will be hard and the progress there likely will be slower in developing than was the progress achieved in

Iraq." Then he added, "Nonetheless, as with Iraq, in Afghanistan, hard is not hopeless."[1] The forces being provided to Afghanistan would be employed by McChrystal in much the same way that Petraeus had directed them in Iraq. Security for the population would be the priority. McChrystal echoed Petraeus's Anaconda strategy from Iraq when he told Congress that, "ultimate success will be the cumulative effect of sustained pressure."[2] In early 2010, major U.S. offensives began and met with initial success. But as everyone expected, the campaign proved very difficult.

By late spring, political rumblings in Washington, D.C., and in the U.S. major media outlets began to sound, highlighting growing frustration that the expected progress was not yet visible. McChrystal worked hard to implement the U.S. COIN strategy; to reduce the number of Afghan civilians who were sometimes harmed by the conduct of military operations; and to ensure that U.S., NATO, and Coalition forces were all working toward a common purpose. McChrystal remained cautiously optimistic and was determined to succeed. Petraeus testified to Congress in mid-June that despite the enormous difficulties posed by the Taliban and their terrorist allies in Afghanistan, sustained U.S. commitment could turn the tide and achieve U.S. objectives.

Then, unexpectedly, a firestorm erupted that led to McChrystal's prompt removal from command by President Obama on June 23, 2010. Several days previously, an article appeared in *Rolling Stone* magazine that contained disparaging remarks that some of McChrystal's personal staff had allegedly made about Vice President Biden, National Security Advisor James Jones, Ambassador Karl Eikenberry, and others. The published comments were widely viewed as disrespectful to the long-standing American tradition of civilian leadership of the armed forces, and many assessed they would ultimately undermine the U.S. leadership of the campaign in Afghanistan. McChrystal immediately apologized and, on President Obama's order, flew to Washington for consultations. During a brief meeting at the White House, the President accepted McChrystal's resignation. A few hours later, President Obama announced that he had asked Petraeus to assume command in Afghanistan and that Petraeus had accepted this new mission.

It was a rare historical moment. Once again, Petraeus found himself in the position of rescuing an American military campaign at a moment of crisis. Sent by a Democratic president to lead the war in Afghanistan, just as several years before he had been sent by a Republican president to take charge of Iraq in its darkest hour, Petraeus once more appeared to the public to be nearly indispensable. His counterinsurgency philosophy already underlay the U.S. effort in Afghanistan, but now Petraeus would personally lead the effort, directing it in detail, from the front lines. He didn't offer any public words on the occasion; he simply accepted the command as his duty.

Petraeus had been all in when he assumed command in Iraq, and he had won at a time when many bet against him. Now, he was embarking on a new mission, and he was wagering everything once more. But this time, despite the tremendous challenges posed by the Afghanistan war, public and private sentiment alike was betting on another win.

NOTES

1. "Petraeus Predicts That Surge Progress in Afghanistan Will Be Slow," *FoxNews.com*, December 9, 2009, http://www.foxnews.com/pol itics/2009/12/09/kerry-underscores-importance-pakistan-war-strategy/.

2. Ibid.

Chapter 21

WHAT PLACE IN HISTORY?

Speaking to a reporter in the months after returning home from commanding the 101st Division in Iraq, Petraeus described what it was like
trying to stay ahead of the near chaos he found in Mosul in 2003, immediately after the fall of Baghdad to U.S. forces:

> We're probably riding really hell-bent for leather here—leaning for-
> ward in the saddle—and it's probably raining sideways, and there's
> lightning bolts out of the sky like that famous Frederick Reming-
> ton print called "Stampede." I have to give credit to an earlier boss
> of mine for that image as well, the great General John—Jack—Gal-
> vin, who used that similar image. I think it's very appropriate to what
> we're doing here. What we're trying to do is just keep it all headed
> in the right direction.[1]

His description is notable because it captures much of the essence of
Petraeus—a man of decisive action who possesses the mental agility to
be comfortable with uncertainty and who reaches into the past to find
wisdom. It took each of these traits, and more, to overcome the insurgency that erupted in Iraq and then to assemble a new national approach

to waging a second counterinsurgency campaign in Afghanistan and the broader Middle East. His success at doing so marks him as the most well-known military figure on today's stage.

But where does Petraeus rank in the historical pantheon of American military leaders? The short answer must be near the top. His career is not yet complete, and so the final entries of his professional record have not yet been entered. From today's vantage point, it seems likely that he is destined for high offices of national service, and hence, his contributions ahead could be even more meaningful than what he has achieved to date. The proof will arrive in the viability of the training methods he has pioneered that are being adopted by the army and its sister services, such as his singular devotion to the intellectual aspects of leader development.

He is for now the preeminent military officer of the 21st century and already stands as both the symbolic, and in many ways, actual leader of his generation of military officers. Better than anyone else, Petraeus has mastered the balance of politics, media, and battlefield success. Uniquely, he is well-known and influential both within and beyond military circles, transcending institutional boundaries that have traditionally limited the reach of any other general officer.

If you turn on a television, or read a magazine or newspaper for any length of time, you will likely encounter commentators eagerly discussing revolutionary changes in sports or the economy or politics. While much of this talk is overheated, in the realm of military affairs, profound changes are indeed underway, changes that Petraeus was quick to note and even quicker to adapt to. While always exhibiting the classic example of the take-charge army officer, he has also dedicated himself to the study of the relationship between armed forces and the societies that create and sustain them.

When Islamist terrorists hijacked U.S. commercial airliners on September 11, 2001, the international security environment changed in profound ways. If World War II demonstrated that the Atlantic and Pacific oceans could no longer keep the nation away from the politics of Europe and Asia, the 9/11 attacks removed any doubt that the American homeland was now a target. Nor as the subsequent wars in Iraq and Afghanistan have shown could the United States always expect to dominate opponents in a quick war. Military leaders must therefore be versatile, innovative, and insightful. Like Petraeus did, they must combine their operational experiences with educational opportunities to broaden their decision-making abilities. Leaders must also operate with a diverse range of allies and international partners. This is a fresh challenge for America's armed forces.

Traditionally, the army has trained leaders by presenting them with simulations of predictable enemy formations. Leaders were taught to consider direct calculations of time and distance and were challenged by compressing either to add stress to training events. Very little consideration was given to helping officers translate tactical situations into operational and strategic objectives or transition from one kind of operation to another. While these methods were successful when the military problem set was defined, now leader training and education must encompass the complexity of social, economic, political, and cultural factors. Such considerations are all the more important because junior leaders are required to make decisions at lower levels of command and will have greater responsibility than ever before. The newest generation of young officers will go forward with this intellectual framework in hand, and if the past is a guide, they will face their own share of challenges on battlefields yet known. While the war in Iraq seems to be drawing down, the fighting in Afghanistan will likely go on for years, challenging Petraeus and those who seek to emulate him alike.

For much of their history, Americans have preferred that there be a clear distinction between war and peace. Petraeus understood early in his career that such a divide is not—in fact, is usually not—possible. He knew that conditions of peace and war almost always exist simultaneously, and that the United States would be unavoidably drawn into such difficult situations. Having witnessed Petraeus's success in Iraq, today's senior army staffs survey the world largely through his vision, a world in which threats are complex, uncertain, and persistent. As an institution, the army is beginning to support the view that many different kinds of enemies will threaten the United States and its interests and allies. Some of these adversaries will employ the conventional tanks and artillery that were familiar during the cold war years, but many others will prefer to employ lightly armed guerrilla cells and use difficult to defend improvised explosive devices (IEDs). Some will even try to explode chemical, biological, or nuclear weapons. Military leaders who can survive and win in this dangerous environment must command in the mold that Petraeus has long advocated. Above all, they must be willing to learn and adapt. As Petraeus told an audience in 2009, explaining the legacy of Vietnam as it applied to future conflict, "The biggest lesson of Vietnam is to not be a prisoner of lessons you may have learned."[2]

Petraeus, of course, didn't alone forecast the changing nature of war, and even he initially underestimated the full extent of the challenges confronting U.S. forces in Iraq. His was a case of underestimating sectarian divisions, something easy to do, even by someone who had studied conflict for decades. In this, Petraeus had much company. But it was Petraeus who regrouped with alacrity and most convincingly led the way to properly define the war in Iraq as one of many dimensions. To engage it winningly, he too led the way across the bridge between the military domain and the worlds of politics and the international media, an accomplishment that places him in the rarefied company of America's most successful military commanders.

In this October 7, 2008, file photo, General David Petraeus speaks at the Association of the U.S. Army annual meeting in Washington. AP Photo/Manuel Balce Ceneta, File.

Few American generals have been able to lay a claim that they succeeded by making a mark beyond uniformed circles in the way that Petraeus now seems to be achieving. In the 19th century, Generals Winfield Scott and Ulysses Grant were strategic leaders who directly and significantly influenced both national policy and military operations. Other well-known commanders were popular, such as Robert E. Lee and Phil Sheridan, but their campaign successes did not translate to enduring changes in the manner that the United States waged war. In the 20th century, General William Pershing decisively orchestrated America's World War I grand strategy, his stature far beyond that of his peers. In World War II, the most famous fighting U.S. general was Lieutenant General George Patton, but Patton never commanded beyond the operational level of war. America's two senior generals were Dwight Eisenhower, who fought in the European theater, and Douglas MacArthur, from the Pacific. Each was the kind of man who was comfortable at the strategic echelon and functioned at the highest levels. Petraeus is not really like either of these men. He certainly exudes MacArthur's confidence and sense of theater, but Petraeus's political savvy is much closer to Eisenhower's steady demeanor and finely balanced diplomatic temperament. In this sense, perhaps Petraeus can be seen as an amalgam of both of these World War II commanders, although the leader that Petraeus himself points to remains Ulysses S. Grant. Petraeus continues to cite that he most admires Grant's determination. He often repeats Grant's words to President Lincoln in 1864, after the Union forces he led had been bloodied during savage fighting in northern Virginia—"I'll fight it out all summer on this line"[3]—as an example of an extraordinary quality for a leader of any rank.

Above all, the question of Petraeus's role points to the larger truth that in many ways, wars never end. They are humankind's most transformative behavior, sweeping away what precedes them and shaping what is to follow. Those killed leave lives interrupted too soon, shattering the dreams of their loved ones. For those who fight and survive, and for those who suffer in war's path, the experience is always too searing to be forgotten. Long after the material debris of combat is put away, cities rebuilt, and civilian occupations resumed, the survivors inevitably continue to refight the battles, their memories, their bodies, and their personal relationships indescribably changed by their experiences. The power and pathos of war even stretches—and sometimes tears—the fabric of nations. So when the last U.S. troops depart Iraq and Afghanistan, the triumphs and tragedies there will stay with the American public as a part of the national psyche. The nation's military and political establishments will no doubt argue for a generation about these wars. Were they worth the cost? Did they make America safer? Which decisions were mistakes, and which led to victory? Reflective people around the world will seek to place America's fights in the context of the broader struggle against terrorism in a world witnessing the rise of great nations like India, China, and Brazil; widespread economic turmoil; and rapidly changing technologies that seem to influence peoples everywhere.

And over time, history, perhaps the sternest judge, will render its verdict too. It is history that will likely view General Petraeus's many achievements through a clear and focused lens. How have his big ideas about waging war in today's complex world kept his troops safe, and how well is America defended wherever he leads them? The answers will have to wait for history's march. But for now, the answer must be very well indeed. Touch wood.

NOTES

1. "Iraq, Afghanistan, and the War on Terror: A Collection of FRONTLINE's Reporting from 9/11 to the Present," *PBS*, *Frontline*, http://www.pbs.org/wgbh/pages/frontline/terror/?utm_campaign=homepage&utm_medium=fixed&utm source=fixed, 8.

2. Thomas Ricks, "Dave Does Dull, Storm Warnings on the Petraeus-ometer," *Foreign Policy*, September 24, 2009, http://ricks.foreignpolicy.com/posts/2009/09/24/dave_does_dull_storm_warnings_on_the_pe traeus_ometer.

3. Bruce Catton, *Grant Takes Command* (Boston: Little Brown, 1968), 223.

SELECTED BIBLIOGRAPHY

Boot, Max. *War Made New: Technology, Warfare, and the Course of History, 1500 to Today.* New York: Gotham Books, 2006.

Bowden, Mark. "David Petraeus's Winning Streak." *Vanity Fair* (online, March 2010), http://www.vanityfair.com/politics/features/2010/05/petraeus-exclusive-201005

Bowden, Mark. "The Professor of War." *Vanity Fair* (online, May 2010), http://www.vanityfair.com/politics/features/2010/05/petraeus-201005

Cloud, David, and Greg Jaffe. *The Fourth Star: Four Generals and the Epic Struggle for the Future of the United States Army.* New York: Crown Publishers, 2009.

Fontenot, Gregory, E. J. Degen, and David Tohn. *On Point: The United States Army in Operation Iraqi Freedom.* Fort Leavenworth, KS: Combat Studies Institute Press, U.S. Army Combined Arms Center, 2004.

Galula, David. *Pacification in Algeria, 1956–1958.* (Originally pub. 1963.) Santa Monica, CA: RAND Corporation, 2006.

Kagan, Frederick W. *Finding the Target: The Transformation of American Military Policy.* New York: Encounter Books, 2006.

Killebrew, Robert B., and David Petraeus. "Winning the Peace: Haiti, the U.S. and the UN." *Armed Forces Journal International* 132, no. 9 (April 1995): 40–41.

PBS, Frontline. *Iraq, Afghanistan, and the War on Terror: A Collection of FRONTLINE's Reporting from 9/11 to the Present.* http://www.pbs.org/wgbh/pages/frontline/terror/?utm campaign=homepage&utm_medium=fixed&utm source=fixed.

Petraeus, David H. "Lessons of History and Lessons of Vietnam." *Parameters* 16, no. 3 (Autumn 1986): 43–53.

Petraeus, David H. "The American Military and the Lessons of Vietnam: A Study of Military Influence and the Use of Force in the Post-Vietnam Era." Princeton, NJ: Princeton University, 1987, OCLC 20673428.

Petraeus, David H. "Military Influence and the Post-Vietnam Use of Force." *Armed Forces & Society* 15, no. 4 (1989): 489–505.

Petraeus, David H. "Beyond the Cloister." *The American Interest* II, no. 6 (July/August 2007): 16–20.

Petraeus, David H. "Battling for Iraq." *Washington Post,* September 26, 2004, http://www.washingtonpost.com/wp-dyn/articles/A49283-2004Sep25.html.

Petraeus, David H. "Learning Counterinsurgency: Observations from Soldiering in Iraq." *Military Review* (January/February 2006). Available online at: http://www.army.mil/professionalwriting/volumes/volume4/april_2006/4_06_2.html.

Ricks, Thomas E. *The Gamble: General David Petraeus and the American Military Adventure in Iraq, 2006–2008.* New York: Penguin Press, 2009.

Robinson, Linda. *Tell Me How This Ends: General David Petraeus and the Search for a Way out of Iraq.* New York: Public Affairs, 2008.

Scales, Robert H., Jr. *Certain Victory: The U.S. Army in the Gulf War.* Washington, DC: Office of the Chief of Staff, U.S. Army, 1993.

U.S. Army. *Field Manual 3-24, Counterinsurgency.* Washington, DC: Headquarters, Department of the Army, December 2006.

Wright, Donald P., and Timothy R. Reese. *On Point II: Transition to the New Campaign, The United States Army in Operation Iraqi Freedom, May 2003–January 2005.* Fort Leavenworth, KS: Combat Studies Institute Press, U.S. Army Combined Arms Center, 2008.

INDEX

About the Author

BRADLEY T. GERICKE earned a commission in armor from the United States Military Academy in 1988. He holds a PhD from Vanderbilt University and is a graduate of the National War College. He has published numerous essays regarding military affairs as well as several college history texts, and he is currently writing *Spearhead: America's Third Armored Division in Peace and War*. His army assignments include duty in the 3d Armored Division in Germany and the Persian Gulf, and in the 2d Infantry Division in Korea. As a strategic plans and policy officer, he has served on the army staff in the Pentagon; at headquarters, Multi-National Force Iraq; and in the Office of the Secretary of Defense for Policy.